WHERE WE STAND

Women Poets on
Literary Tradition

WHERE WE STAND

Women Poets on Literary Tradition

EDITED AND WITH
AN INTRODUCTION BY
SHARON BRYAN

W. W. NORTON & COMPANY
New York • London

Composition by Graphics Composition, Athens, Georgia.
Manufacturing by Courier Companies.

Library of Congress Cataloging-in-Publication Data
Where we stand : women poets on literary tradition / edited and with
an introduction by Sharon Bryan.
p.   cm.
1. American poetry—Women authors—History and criticism—Theory, etc.
2. American poetry—20th century—History and criticism—Theory, etc.
3. Women and literature—United States—History—20th century.
4. Influence (Literary, artistic, etc.) I. Bryan, Sharon.
PS151.W4   1993
811'.54099287—dc20   93-11533

ISBN 0-393-03570-2

W. W. Norton & Comapny, Inc., 500 Fifth Avenue, New York, N.Y. 10110
W. W. Norton & Company Ltd., 10 Coptic Street, London WC1A 1PU

1 2 3 4 5 6 7 8 9 0

CONTENTS

INTRODUCTION

Sharon Bryan

The idea for this collection of essays arose out my own confusions on the topic of gender and poetry. Over the years I tried to write something that would help me clarify my thoughts and feelings, but whenever I began I was overcome by conflicting impulses: on the one hand, gender was irrelevant to art; on the other, I kept bumping up against differences and disparities.

Many women poets I know are similarly of two—or more— minds. Most who are my generation and older, certainly, grew up reading far more poems by men than by women. Male poets were our models, and the occasional women poets were clearly the exception rather than the rule. I didn't see anything odd about that at the time, and for many years I argued that poetry—indeed, any of the arts—did and should supersede questions of gender. I admired Elizabeth Bishop's refusal to publish work in all-women anthologies or magazine issues, and adhered to the same principle myself. That was how I thought of it: a matter of principle.

Yet all along, from the time I began to read contemporary poetry seriously, beginning in the late 1960s, I had experiences that ran counter to this position. One of the first anthologies I owned was *Poems of our Moment*, edited by John Hollander. I remember how disappointed I was to discover that only three of the thirty- four poets included were women. I also remember reading through those poems—by Rich, Plath, and Swenson—first. I wasn't equally moved by all of them, of course, but I was drawn by voices that were new to me and yet at the same time familiar. Even then, apparently, I sensed that I needed something—models, examples, emotions, attitudes—not represented by the predomi- nantly male tradition I knew.

Sharon Bryan ✷

Still, the two tracks continued to be separate: on the one hand I wanted to believe that gender was irrelevant to my life and work as a poet; on the other, the evidence continued to accumulate that I and other women writers inevitably have a different relationship to a primarily male literary tradition from that of male poets. How, for example, are we to read poems that treat women as goddesses, as temptresses, as symbols? How are we to read essays and criticism that assume all poets are male?

When I was in graduate school, I heard some male teachers speak dismissively of poems about domestic subjects as "women's poetry." After many years of teaching, I continue to hear women students describe male teachers who say, apologetically, that they don't know how to talk about "women's poems." (I can't conceive of refusing to comment on a male student's poems on similar grounds.)

Citing Elizabeth Bishop's example, I declined to submit work to publications devoted exclusively to poetry by women, but when I looked for anthologies to use in classes, none offered a representative selection of poetry by women. Eventually I added to my reading lists some of those very collections I had earlier criticized.

Several years ago a friend and I were discussing a recent book of poems that had received very favorable reviews. We admired the craftsmanship of the poems, but also felt distanced in some way from their attitudes toward literary history. My friend described the dilemma perfectly: she said that she couldn't help but be impressed by the author's wide-ranging familiarity with western literary tradition, but that she both envied and resented the ease with which he seemed to take that tradition, and his own place in it, for granted.

This is the heart of the matter: many women poets have begun their writing lives assuming that they were part of an ongoing tradition, and then gradually revised their sense of what that meant after persistent reminders that the tradition didn't necessarily return the favor. *We* might prefer not to think about gender, to concentrate on other matters, but incidents and circumstances keep reminding us of it.

One poet I invited to contribute said she didn't see that there was any issue to discuss and asked if, for example, some women really feel left out when they read Keats. As it happened, I had been reading some of Keats's odes, with enormous pleasure and empathy. Then, just the night before, I had come across a passage in one of his letters to a close friend. Fatigued by his own obsessive labors, he confides that he "sometimes can't help envying women, because they have no imagination." This comment won't compromise my pleasure in reading the odes, but for a moment it took my breath away, as if someone had thrown cold water in my face. Apparently his negative capability extended only so far.

When I had grown weary of listening to the voices in my own head repeat the same disputes without getting anywhere, I realized that what I really wanted to do was hear how other women thought about these issues. Thus, this collection.

I wrote to almost eighty women poets, describing the project and inviting them to contribute. In my letter I cited T. S. Eliot's influential essay, "Tradition and the Individual Talent," in which he spells out the poet's relationship to the poetry that preceded him. He refers throughout to the poet as "he," and I asked the poets I wrote to if they felt left out by that. I also quoted Adrienne Rich: "We need to know the writing of the past, and know it differently than we have ever known it, not to pass on a tradition but to break its hold over us," and asked if they agreed or disagreed. I also asked if they thought they could have the same relationship to literary tradition as their male counterparts; if their responses to a male poet's work were affected by the way women appeared in those poems; and whether they were equally drawn to poems by men and by women. I pointed out the obvious, that teaching passes on attitudes toward literary tradition, and that publishing reflects and shapes those attitudes, and asked them to consider their own experiences in those areas. I asked if they had both women and men as poetry teachers, and if they thought it mattered. I asked how they felt about women-only publications. I also urged them not to feel limited by my questions, but to approach the topic however they liked.

The response was immediate and gratifying. Many of those who accepted expressed feelings similar to my own: the issues had been nagging at them for years, and they were grateful for a chance to focus their thoughts. Many of those who declined did so reluctantly, citing the pressure of other deadlines. Some who originally declined wrote a week or two later to say that they hadn't been able to stop thinking about the questions and would indeed write something after all. Those who accepted took the matter very much to heart, and their essays are thoughtful, thought-provoking, and moving. They are serious engagements—often tempered by humor—with complex questions.

I wanted to represent as wide an age range as possible, in part to see if there are recognizable differences between generations. I also wanted to represent as many viewpoints as possible, from poets who would describe themselves as feminists to those who believe that gender is secondary when it comes to reading and writing poetry. I invited poets with a range of backgrounds and experiences.

The results are more diverse than I could have imagined—like snowflakes, no two alike. Where do we stand? All over the map. The essays don't lend themselves to generalizations or categories. The common ground is that the writers are women and poets, but from there they strike out in many different directions.

All the poets here are working to locate themselves on a map that is constantly being redrawn. When Pound said, "Make it new," he could take for granted that he and his fellow poets all agreed about what "it" was. Now it's often the very antecedent of the pronoun that's being called into question. Many of the writers here think in terms of a greatly expanded definition of tradition, or of traditions, plural.

From the time we are born, we try to discover where we stand in relationship to the world around us: we call out and listen for what comes back, we see ourselves reflected in the way the world responds to us. It's not surprising that many of the essays here recount pivotal experiences that prompted the writers to revise their sense of themselves, of literary tradition, or both.

All of the essays here deal in one way or another with women poets and literary tradition, but they focus on different elements of that intersection. Some concentrate on the role of gender, some on aspects of literary tradition, and others on the interplay between the two.

Martha Collins begins at the beginning, with our earliest experiences of language. She argues that the language we speak is irrevocably the "mother tongue," since we all hear it first from our mothers. Pattiann Rogers stresses the central importance of her role as a mother of two sons, then goes on to point out how few women writers have also been mothers, and how little poetry is about the experience of mothering. Gwen Head offers a sketch of the essay she had expected to write, on the progress women have made in recent years, then describes how that was derailed by her visit to the Museum of Women and Automata in Paris. Beginning with incidents from childhood and proceeding through marriage, motherhood, and academic life, Judith Kitchen presents a series of telling episodes through which she defined herself as a woman and a poet. Amy Clampitt describes setting out to write poems when Edna St. Vincent Millay was one of the few women poets whose work received serious attention. Lisel Mueller ascribes her sense of the relative unimportance of gender in art to the attitudes of her intellectual parents and her upbringing in Germany; only after she came to America did she become aware of gender as a potential shaping—and limiting—factor. Arguing against seeing gender as a primary factor in art, Anne Stevenson makes a useful distinction between the social realm, where "inequalities of opportunity still exist," and the literary, where, ". . . in all ways that matter, what goes for men goes for women." Cynthia Macdonald points out that boys and girls have different tasks growing up: boys leave their mothers but find a similar figure in female lovers, while girls leave their mothers for a male lover. "Thus," she says, "the boy has one primary figure in his life . . . but the girl has two." She goes on to speculate that something analogous is true for male and female poets.

Those essays that focus on literary tradition come at it from various angles. Grace Schulman reminds us that we are often influenced unconsciously, by something we *can't* name, and offers as example Walt Whitman's encounters with Judaic traditions. Alicia Ostriker describes her attraction to William Blake's work, and how her relationship to it has been modified over time by her increasing awareness of the importance of gender. Joy Harjo brings to her work a powerful sense of other traditions, especially from her Muscogee background, which greatly broadens our sense of literary history and the sources of poetry. Brenda Hillman describes ways her work has been enriched by her study of a range of examples, including Gnostic texts. Deborah Tall recounts her resistance to the notion of a single literary tradition, and concludes that "if we owe literary tradition anything, it's our conscious revision of it." Carol Muske says it's the future we must revise, since as things stand women poets must face the future without the benefit of a "literary trust fund." Debora Greger's commentary on tradition is a terse, pointed collage featuring Walt Whitman and Emily Dickinson.

Those writers who concentrate on the relationship between women poets and literary tradition delineate ways those two elements have shaped and redefined one another. Eavan Boland describes her own struggle with the weight of Irish literary history, and its mythologized images of women, and how her recognition of the gap between those images and actual Irish women led her to explore that territory in her poems. Kathleen Fraser recounts gradually finding herself on the margins of the traditional literary map, and then redefining her position as the center of a different tradition, one in which being a *woman* writer is the defining element. Suzanne Matson disputes the notion that the pronoun "he" can stand for "everyone," and argues that we must "reclaim the universal" so that it includes women as well as men. Colleen McElroy describes the gradual process of learning to write poems that would be true to her own experiences as a black woman writer, and the absence of any reflection of those experiences in the poetry she was taught in school. Madeline DeFrees analyzes the several kinds of mirrors to which women writers can look as they shape their identities: the mirror of tradition, the role model mirror, the mirror of criticism, and the specific example of Virginia Woolf's mirror. Maxine Kumin recounts what it was like to begin writing poetry in the 1950s, as a suburban housewife. Wendy Battin's essay reflects the necessarily fragmentary nature of any maps we make of the literary landscape, and the provisional nature of where we stand in relation to them.

Although many anthologies of women's work have appeared in recent years, and books about women writers, I don't know of any other collection like this one, where women writers specifically address questions of gender and literary tradition. The intensity and complexity of the responses here indicate that the writers have been mulling the issues—to themselves, if not aloud—for a long time, and that these questions touch deep chords. So why the long silence? Why hasn't there already been more open discussion of these topics, especially at a time when women's studies programs and feminist criticism would seem to provide a supportive context in which to air them?

I can think of several reasons. For one, poetry not only acknowledges but celebrates ambiguity, nuance, doubt, and paradox, so most poets are distrustful of any "isms" that seem to offer certainty, or to put politics before poetry. Some feminist rhetoric seems to reduce complex issues to a matter of choosing sides, and neither position could do justice to the thoughts and feelings involved. I think many women poets have been reluctant to voice their concerns because they were afraid of being misunderstood, labelled, pigeonholed, dismissed. The first drafts of some of these essays were tentative, hesitant, and apologetic for any expressions of anger or frustration. But gradually the voices became steadier, more confident, and more matter-of-fact as the writers found ways to articulate the full range of their thoughts and feelings. Women poets are also aware of the practical realities: most positions of influence over literary careers, from publishing to reviewing to prize-giving, are still held by men, and women poets are reluctant to offend men who have helped them or are in a position to do so.

The writers whose essays are included here fought through a thicket of similar doubts and difficulties to get their thoughts on paper, to discover what they think and feel by putting it into words. Reading the essays, individually and as a group, I am extremely moved by their candor and insight. Thanks to the hard work of the contributors, and to the serious engagement they brought to the project, I have finally been able to hear how some other women writers think about these difficult questions. I am reaffirmed and heartened by accounts that mirror my own experiences, and enlightened by those that are different. One of the most important elements in my life as a writer has always been my sense

Sharon Bryan ✒

of community with other writers, of shared tasks and sensibilities. Now I have an equally powerful feeling of belonging to a community of women writers.

I originally objected to using the phrase "woman poets" in the title of this collection. I argued against it on the grounds that it represented a diminishment, a hyphenation, something partial, a qualification of the more complete term *poet*, that it was nothing more than an updated version of the ghastly "poetess." But I have come to see, reading these essays as a group, how the phrase can instead be an addition, an expansion, a whole, a crucial and accurate balance. It is also a simple acknowledgement of fact: woman/poet. Whatever answers we come to, I think the question of how those two elements are related in our lives and work is inescapable. Men, too, will have to acknowledge gender as a shaping force in art—which will expand the possibilities for their work, as well. They haven't had to do so in the past only because literary tradition and *male* literary tradition were virtually synonymous. I think many younger women writers may *begin* by assuming their outsider status in relation to what they see as one among multiple traditions, and so feel less conflict and confusion than those of us who learned to think in terms of a single club to which we did or didn't belong. I hope that the essays in *Where We Stand* will serve as the beginning of a many-sided conversation.

In addition to the contributors, I would also like to thank our editor at Norton, Jill Bialosky. She has been an enthusiastic supporter of the collection since I first proposed it to her, and her efforts on its behalf have made the book a reality.

Finally, I want to thank my two editorial assistants on *River City*, J. P. Craig and Joey Flamm. I literally could not have gotten this book to press without their substantial help.

WHERE WE STAND

Women Poets on
Literary Tradition

SUBTERRANEAN MAPS: A POET'S CARTOGRAPHY

Wendy Battin

> . . . *we are such unconscious people. . .*[1]
> T. S. Eliot
>
> *The map is not the territory.*[2]
> A. Korzybski

1.

For all the years I lived in Boston, I had no car. My map of the greater city radiated from the black-on-white T's that marked the subway entrances: from Harvard and Kendall Squares, from Haymarket, from Government Center, the known world bloomed, the grid of streets filled in with shops and smog, corners where the balky *Don't Walk* signs had left me idling. The rest of my geography was underground. "How do I get to Newbury Street?" yelled a tourist, panicked in the mayhem of Storrow Drive. I couldn't help.

My map of literature is much the same. At fourteen I stumbled into a few poems by Ezra Pound; his London metro let me off in China, where I emerged into the sunlight of Lao-tse and Li Po. And from Pound I followed the trail of dropped names to *The Waste Land*, and on to Yeats and Stevens. I opened a paperback anthology to "Thirteen Ways of Looking at a Blackbird," and read,

> I do not know which to prefer,
> The beauty of inflections
> Or the beauty of innuendoes,

The blackbird whistling
Or just after.

It shocked me into silence, then into words: *I didn't know you could say that.* I went on writing my fourteen-year-old's doggerel, but I knew that somewhere on the other side of it I might find a way to *that.* Because language could do that, could break the loneliness of being conscious, could translate the buzz of perception into a call-and-response.

What Stevens gave me in that moment was the knowledge that I was real, that the sparks and shifts of my own mind happened in other minds, and that they had value in being shared. It was admission not to the private club of "literature," but to the human family.

My own map is larger now, starred by other shocks of recognition, by countless other writers who have shown me how to continue. But the tradition I write from is still an artifact of my loneliness; in the white noise of television, of language made senseless by political lies and the lies of buying and selling, Shakespeare carries no more authority than Dickinson, than Han Shan or Akhmatova. I'm often angry that more women's voices have not been saved. I'm often amazed and grateful that any truthful voices have been saved at all.

If you bring me a cup of water in the desert, I will not ask whether you are male or female, whether you come from Paris or from Lagos. I could even conceive some nostalgia for the coherence of a central tradition, whether it wanted to admit me or not; but it would be too willful an invention, too chimerical and narrow to be convincing.

2.

Chimera:
—*a mythological fire-breathing monster, commonly represented with a lion's head, a goat's body, and a serpent's tail.*

—*Genetics: an organism composed of two or more genetically distinct tissues, as an organism that is partly male and partly female, or an artificially produced individual having tissues of several species.*[3]

The only tradition I know is not a thing, but a process; not something we have, but something we do. My tradition as a poet is the sense I make of my being human, and the craft of that making; and, as "making sense" is a statement about order and value, i.e., about relationship, I make it from the sense that others have made. I make *myself*, continually, from the sense that other human beings have made. But for all my conjuring, the blank spaces on my map expand more rapidly than the map does; maps from other cultures, from physics, linguistics, anthropology, from the homeless women I cook for and from the Taoist priest who teaches me martial arts, overlie my own and transform it. What else is it to be alive, in the chaos of the present?

And with whom will we commit our acts of tradition? I've recited a few stanzas of Yeats to a woman whose only address beyond "the street" is a psychiatric ward. Later she shouted to me from her corner, "Love is like the lion's tooth!" She knew what it meant. The shoppers scattered; Yeats, I think, would have been pleased.

3.

Whoever has approved this idea of order. . . will not find it preposterous that the past should be altered by the present as much as the present is directed by the past.
T. S. Eliot

My own historical sense includes the ebb and flow of feminist thought; I'm not disturbed that John Donne failed to recognize the full humanity of women, any more than I fault him for not including quantum mechanics in his world view. I am deeply disturbed when I encounter the same blindness in my contemporaries.

When I was an undergraduate in the early seventies, Sylvia Plath was the popular icon of the woman poet, and one day we heard that Anne Sexton had committed suicide. That night, at a party, a male professor cornered me and asked, "Why do all you women poets kill yourselves?" I was twenty years old, awed by the real talent and knowledge of my teachers. I didn't say, "Because of people like you." I felt some of the anger and fear he might have intended me to feel; I felt even more the epistemological shock I've felt dealing with some schizophrenics, when a rift opens in their seemingly lucid speech and reveals the alien logic behind it.

Plath's mythographers, who claimed that she bartered her sanity for moments of genius, were spinning out a strand of Western literary tradition: Art at the price of Life, the Faust-haunted usury of spirit that admits of nothing that can't be traded and sold. I would not dispense with Goethe, who knew better; his Faust awakens from economics into *grace*, a word that even the most life-loathing monks had to learn from the body. But add the unconscious authority of that metaphor to the belief—equally unconscious?—that a woman has no right to poetry, and the resulting potion can be lethal.

But that's a use the living make of even the most eloquent dead; it's also more dangerously a use the dead—from their home in our underworld of hatreds and habits, inherited fears and loves—make of the living. Had that professor been momentarily hypnotized by some other theme, equally deep in his tradition—say, the artist as outsider—the news of a poet's death might have led him elsewhere. He might have chosen, if the same mood was on him, to threaten me as an artist rather than as a woman. That would have been, oddly, a more personal attack, and much less incongruous. The intellectual tradition we share includes detailed observations of primate social hierarchies and territorial drives, and even then I knew an aspiring alpha male when I saw one. We at least would have recognized each other as players on the same field, however unpleasant the game might be.

All the same, I beg his pardon for abstracting him into an icon in his turn—"nothing personal," I could tell him, to cover both my crime and my alibi, a sort of knee-jerk justice. He was a man having a bad day, perhaps; perhaps his bad days come less often now. And none of this map-making is of any use if the map forgets the territory, if the idea *human* abandons the changeable fumbling human. What Adrienne Rich once invoked as a "common language" must be, in the linear way of words, an intimate contract—I speak to you, you speak to me. Weave those numberless intimacies into a *shared* tradition and we have a Commons, that open field where the living can take up space and move freely, as the living must.

4.

...we know not why we go upstairs, or why we come down again, our most daily movements are like the passage of a ship on an unknown sea, and the sailors at the masthead ask, pointing their glasses to the horizon, Is there land or is there none? to which, if we are prophets, we make answer "Yes"; if we are truthful we say "No."[4]

Because I know that my map is provisional, that I have pieced it together out of my own need, I am baffled when I encounter the guardians of any tradition who do not know that their maps are also partial, their historical sense equally sporadic. I have met scholars still unruffled by cybernetics in the nineties, who can base their lectures to the young on the assumption that the Cartesian duality, the divorce of mind from matter, is a law of nature; "secular" critics so xenophobic that they can attack a Zen-based work on "intellectual grounds," because it offends their unconscious Judaeo-Christian cosmology. When those premises go unchallenged, finally, I feel the same rifts opening, the same breach of trust among the living.

My own blind spots must be of similar magnitude. And so I end up embracing the chaos, the cultural relativism of maps stacking up, and fragments of maps. The early disorienting strangeness I felt, as a woman, as a member of the wrong class or caste, when I was confronted with the Monuments of Culture, has become for me, by now, an essential strangeness; I couldn't trust myself without it. I imagine any tradition that can hold both William Blake and Byron in a single thought can surely accommodate us as well. But it no longer surprises me when I'm taken for the barbarian at the gates—or for the cleaning lady at her subway stop. She's sometimes who I am.

NOTES

1. "Tradition and the Individual Talent," p. 37 [originally published in 1920; all page references here and in subsequent essays are to: *Selected Prose of T. S. Eliot*, ed. Frank Kermode (New York: Harcourt Brace Jovanovich and Farrar Straus Giroux), pp. 37-47.—Ed.]

2. Alfred Korzybski, *Science and Sanity* (New York: Science Press, 1941), p. 58.

3. *Random House Dictionary of the English Language* (New York, 1969), p. 234.

4. Virginia Woolf, *Orlando* (New York: Harcourt Brace Jovanovich), p. 78.

OUTSIDE HISTORY

Eavan Boland

Years ago, I went to the Isle of Achill for Easter. I was a student at Trinity then and I had the loan of a friend's cottage. It was a one-storey stone building with two rooms and a view of sloping fields.

April was cold that year. The cottage was in sight of the Atlantic and at night a bitter, humid wind blew across the shore. By day there was heckling sunshine but after dark a fire was necessary. The loneliness of the place suited me. My purposes in being there were purgatorial and I had no intention of going out and about. I had done erratically, to say the least, in my first-year exams. In token of the need to do better, I had brought with me a small, accusing volume of the court poets of the Silver Age. In other words, those sixteenth-century English song writers, like Wyatt and Raleigh, whose lines appear so elegant, so offhand, yet whose poems smell of the gallows.

I was there less than a week. The cottage had no water and every evening the caretaker, an old woman who shared a cottage with her brother at the bottom of the field, would carry water up to me. I can see her still. She has a tea-towel round her waist— perhaps this is one image that has become all the images I have of her—she wears an old cardigan and her hands are blushing with cold as she puts down the bucket. Sometimes we talk inside the door of the cottage. Once, I remember, we stood there as the dark grew all around us and I could see stars beginning to curve in the stream behind us.

She was the first person to talk to me about the famine. The first person, in fact, to speak to me with any force about the terrible parish of survival and death which the event had been in those regions. She kept repeating to me that they were great people, the people in the famine. Great people. I had never heard that before. She pointed out the beauties of the place. But they themselves, I see now, were a subtext. On the eastern side of Keel, the cliffs of Menawn rose sheer out of the water. And here was Keel itself, with its blond strand and broken stone, where the villages in the famines, she told me, had moved closer to the shore, the better to eat the seaweed.

Memory is treacherous. It confers meanings which are not apparent at the time. I want to say that I understood this woman as emblem and instance of everything I am about to propose. Of course I did not. Yet even then I sensed a power in the encounter. I knew, without having words for it, that she came from a past which affected me. When she pointed out Keel to me that evening when the wind was brisk and cold and the light was going—when she gestured towards that shore which had stones as outlines and monuments of a desperate people—what was she pointing at? History? A nation? Her memories or mine?

Those questions, once I began to write my own poetry, came back to haunt me. "I have been amazed, more than once, " wrote Helen Cixous, "by a description a woman gave me of a world all her own, which she had been secretly haunting since early childhood." As the years passed, my amazement grew. I would see again the spring evening, the woman talking to me. Above all, I would remember how, when I finished speaking to her, I went in, lit a fire, took out my book of English court poetry and memorized all over again—with no sense of irony or omission—the cadences of power and despair.

I have written this to probe the virulence and necessity of the idea of a nation. Not on its own and not in a vacuum, but as it intersects with a specific poetic inheritance and as that inheritance, in turn, cut across me as woman and poet. Some of these intersections are personal. Some of them may be painful to remember. Nearly all of them are elusive and difficult to describe with any degree of precision. Nevertheless, I believe these intersections, if I can observe them at all properly here, reveal something about poetry, about nationalism, about the difficulties for a woman poet within a constraining national tradition. Perhaps the argument itself is nothing more than a way of revisiting the cold lights of that western evening and the force of that woman's conversation. In any case, the questions inherent in that encounter remain with me. It could well be that they might appear, even to a sympathetic reader, too complex to admit of any answer. In other words, that an argument like mine must contain too many imponderables to admit of any practical focus.

Yet I have no difficulty in stating the central premise of my argument. It is that over a relatively short time—certainly no more than a generation or so—women have moved from being the subjects and objects of Irish poems to being the authors of them. It is a momentous transit. It is also a disruptive one. It raises questions of identity, issues of poetic motive and ethical direction which can seem almost impossibly complex. What is more, such a transit—like the slow course of a star or the shifts in a constellation—is almost invisible to the naked eye. Critics may well miss it or map it inaccurately. Yet such a transit inevitably changes our idea of measurement, of distance, of the past as well as the future. Most importantly, it changes our idea of the Irish poem; of its composition and authority, of its right to appropriate certain themes and make certain fiats. And, since poetry is never local for long, that in turn widens out into further implications.

Everything I am about to argue here could be taken as local and personal, rooted in one country and one poetic inheritance; and both of them mine. Yet, if the names were changed, if situations and places were transposed, the issues might well be revealed as less parochial. This is not, after all, an essay on the craft of the art. I am not writing about aesthetics but about the ethics which are altogether less visible in a poetic tradition. Who the poet is, what he or she nominates as a proper theme for poetry, what self he or she discovers and confirms through this subject matter—all of this involves an ethical choice. The more volatile the material—and a wounded history, public or private, is always volatile—the more intensely ethical the choice. Poetic ethics are evident and urgent in any culture where tensions between a poet and his or her birthplace are inherited and established. Poets from such cultures might well recognize some of the issues raised here. After all, this is not the only country or the only politic where the previously passive objects of a work of art have, in a relatively short time, become the authors of it

So it is with me. For this very reason, early on as a poet,

certainly in my twenties, I realized that the Irish nation as an existing construct in Irish poetry was not available to me. I would not have been able to articulate it at that point, but at some preliminary level I already knew that the anguish and power of that woman's gesture on Achill, with its suggestive hinterland of pain, was not something I could predict or rely on in Irish poetry. There were glimpses here and there; sometimes more than that. But all too often, when I was searching for such an inclusion, what I found was rhetoric or imagery which alienated me: a fusion of the national and the feminine which seemed to simplify both.

It was not a comfortable realization. There was nothing clear-cut about my feelings. I had tribal ambivalences and doubts; and even then I had an uneasy sense of the conflict which awaited me. On the one hand I knew that, as a poet, I could not easily do without the idea of a nation. Poetry in every time draws on that reserve. On the other, I could not as a woman accept the nation formulated for me by Irish poetry and its traditions. At one point it even looked to me as if the whole thing might be made up of irreconcilable differences. At the very least, it seemed to me that I was likely to remain an outsider in my own national literature, cut off from its archive, at a distance from its energy. Unless, that is, I could repossess it. This essay is about that conflict and that repossession, and about the fact that repossession itself is not a static or single act. Indeed this essay, which describes it, may itself be no more than a part of it.

A nation. It is, in some ways, the most fragile and improbable of concepts. Yet the idea of an Ireland, resolved and healed of its wounds, is an irreducible presence in the Irish past and its literature. In one sense, of course, both the concept and its realization resist definition. It is certainly nothing conceived in what Edmund Burke called "the spirit of rational liberty." When a people have been so dispossessed by event as the Irish in the eighteenth and nineteenth centuries an extra burden falls on the very idea of a nation. What should be a political aspiration becomes a collective fantasy. The dream itself becomes freighted with invention. The Irish nation, materializing in the songs and ballads of these centuries, is a sequence of improvised images. These songs, these images, wonderful and terrible and memorable as they are, propose for a nation an impossible task: to be at once an archive of defeat and a diagram of victory.

As a child I loved these songs. Even now, in some moods and at certain times, I can find it difficult to resist their makeshift angers. And no wonder. The best of them are written—like the lyrics of Wyatt and Raleigh—within sight of the gibbet. They breathe just free of the noose.

In one sense I was a captive audience. My childhood was spent in London. My image-makers as a child, therefore, were refractions of my exile: conversations overheard, memories and visitors. I listened and absorbed. For me, as for many another exile, Ireland was my nation long before it was once again my country. That nation, then and later, was a session of images: of defeats and sacrifices, of individual defiances happening off-stage. The songs enhanced the images; the images reinforced the songs. To me they were the soundings of the place I had lost: drowned treasure.

It took me years to shake off those presences. In the end, though, I did escape. My escape was assisted by the realization that these songs were effect not cause. They were only the curators of the dream; not the inventors. In retrospect I could accuse both them and the dream of certain cruel simplifications. I made then, as I make now, a moral division between what those songs sought to accomplish and what Irish poetry must seek to achieve. The songs, with their postures and their angers, glamourized resistance, action. But the Irish experience, certainly for the purposes of poetry, was only incidentally about action and resistance. At a far deeper level—and here the Achill woman returns—it was about defeat. The coffin ships, the soup queues, those desperate villagers at the shoreline—these things had actually happened. The songs, persuasive, hypnotic, could wish them away. Poetry could not. Of course the relation between a poem and a past is never that simple. When I met the Achill woman I was already a poet, I thought of myself as a poet. Yet nothing that I understood about poetry enabled me to understand her better. Quite the reverse. I turned my back on her in that cold twilight and went to commit to memory the songs and artifices of the very power systems which had made her own memory such an archive of loss.

If I understand her better now, and my relation to her, it is not just because my sense of irony or history has developed over the years; although I hope that they have. It is more likely because of my own experience as a poet. Inevitably, any account of this carrries the risk of subjective codes and impressions. Yet, in poetry in particular and women's writing in general, the private witness is often all there is to go on. Since my personal experience as a poet is part of my source material, it is to that I now turn.

I entered Trinity to study English and Latin. Those were the early sixties and Dublin was another world—a place for which I can still feel Henry James's "tiger-pounce of homesickness." In a very real sense it was a city of images and anachronisms. There were still brewery horses on Grafton Street, their rumps draped and smoking under sackcloth. In the coffee bars, they poached eggs in a rolling boil and spooned them onto thick, crustless toasts. The lights went on at twilight; by midnight the city was full of echoes.

After the day's lectures, I took a bus home from College. It was short journey. Home was an attic flat on the near edge of a town that was just beginning to sprawl. There in the kitchen, on an oilskin tablecloth, I wrote my first real poems: derivative, formalist, gesturing poems. I was a very long way from Adrienne Rich's realization that "instead of poems about experience, I am getting poems that are experiences." If anything, my poems were other people's experiences. This, after all, was the heyday of the Movement in Britain, and the neat stanza, the well-broken line, were the very stuff of poetic identity.

Now I wonder how many young women poets taught themselves—in rooms like that, with a blank discipline—to write the poem that was in the air, rather than the one within their experience? How many faltered, as I did, not for lack of answers, but for lack of questions? "It will be a long time still, I think," wrote Virginia Woolf, "before a woman can sit down to write a book without finding a phantom to be slain, a rock to be dashed against."

But for now, let me invent a shift of time. I am turning down those streets which echo after midnight. I am climbing the stairs of a coffee bar which stays open late. I know what I will find. Here is the salt-glazed mug on a table-top which is as scarred as a desk in a country school. Here is the window with its view of an empty street, of lamplight and iron. And there, in the corner, is my younger self.

I draw up a chair, I sit down opposite her. I begin to talk—no, to harangue her. Why, I say, do you do it? Why do you go back to that attic flat, night after night, to write in forms explored and sealed by English men hundreds of years ago? You are Irish. You are a woman. Why do you keep these things at the periphery of the poem? Why do you not move them to the center, where they belong?

But the woman who looks back at me is uncomprehending. If she answers at all it will be with the rhetoric of a callow apprenticeship: that the poem is pure process, that the technical encounter is the one which guarantees all others. She will speak about the dissonance of the line and the necessity for the stanza. And so on.

"For what is the poet responsible?" asked Allen Tate. "He is responsible for the virtue proper to him as a poet, for his special *arête*: for the mastery of a disciplined language which will not shun the full report of the reality conveyed to him by his awareness."

She is a long way, that young woman—with her gleaming cup and her Movement jargon—from the full report of anything. In her lack of any sense of implication or complication, she might as well be a scientist in the thirties, bombarding uranium with neutrons.

If I try now to analyze why such a dialogue would be a waste of time, I come up with several reasons. One of them is that it would take years for me to see, let alone comprehend, certain realities. Not until the oilskin tablecloth was well folded and the sprawling town had become a rapacious city, and the attic flat was a house in the suburbs, could I accept the fact that I was a woman and a poet in a culture which had the greatest difficulty associating the two ideas. "A woman must often take a critical stance towards her social, historical and cultural position in order to experience her own quest," wrote the American poet and feminist Rachel Blau de Plessis. "Poems of the self's growth, or of self-knowledge, may often include or be preceded by a questioning of major social presciptions about the shape women's experience should take." In years to come, I would never be sure whether my poems had generated the questions or the questions had facilitated the poems. All that lay ahead. "No poet," said Eliot, "no artist of any kind has his complete meaning alone." In the meantime, I existed whether I liked it or not in mesh, a web, a labyrinth of associations. Of poems past and present. Contemporary poems. Irish poems.

Irish poetry was predominantly male. Here or there you found a small eloquence, like "After Aughrim" by Emily Lawless. Now and again, in discussion, you heard a woman's name. But the lived vocation, the craft witnessed by a human life—that was missing. And I missed it. Not in the beginning, perhaps. But later, when perceptions of womanhood began to redirect my own work, what I regretted was the absence of an expressed poetic life which would have dignified and revealed mine. The influence of absences should not be underestimated. Isolation itself can have a powerful effect in the life of a young writer. "I'm talking about real influence now," says Raymond Carver. "I'm talking about the moon and the tide."

I turned to the work of Irish male poets. After all, I thought of myself as an Irish poet. I wanted to locate myself within the Irish poetic tradition. The dangers and stresses in my own themes gave me an added incentive to discover a context for them. But what I found dismayed me.

The majority of Irish male poets depended on women as motifs in their poetry. They moved easily, deftly, as if by right among images of women in which I did not believe and of which I could not approve. The women in their poems were often passive, decorative, raised to emblematic status. This was especially true where the woman and the idea of the nation were mixed: where the nation became a woman and the woman took on a national posture.

The trouble was these images did good service as ornaments. In fact they had a wide acceptance as ornaments by readers of Irish poetry. Women in such poems were frequently referred to approvingly as mythic, emblematic. But to me these passive and simplified women seemed a corruption. Moreover, the transaction they urged on the reader, to accept them as mere decoration, seemed to compound the corruption. For they were not decorations, they were not ornaments. However distorted these images, they had their roots in a suffered truth.

What had happened? How had the women of our past—the women of a long struggle and a terrible survival—undergone such a transformation? How had they suffered Irish history and in-

scribed themselves in the speech and memory of the Achill woman, only to re-emerge in Irish poetry as fictive queens and national sybils?

The more I thought about it, the more uneasy I became. The
wrath and grief of Irish history seemed to me—as it did to many—
one of our true possessions. Women were part of that wrath, had
endured that grief. It seemed to me a species of human insult that
at the end of all, in certain Irish poems, they should become elements of style rather than aspects of truth.

The association of the feminine and the national—and the con-
sequent simplification of both—is not of course a monopoly of
Irish poetry. "All my life," wrote Charles de Gaulle, "I have
thought about France in a certain way. The emotional side of me
tends to imagine France like the princess in the fairy-tale, or the
Madonna of the Frescoes." De Gaulle's words point up the power
of nationhood to edit the reality of womanhood. Once the idea of a
nation influences the perception of a woman, then that woman is
suddenly and inevitably simplified. She can no longer have complex feelings and aspirations. She becomes the passive projection
of a national idea.

Irish poems simplified women most at the point of intersection
between womanhood and Irishness. The further the Irish poem
drew away from the idea of Ireland, the more real and persuasive
became the images of women. Once the pendulum swung back the
simplifications started again. The idea of the defeated nation being
reborn as a triumphant woman was central to a certain kind of Irish
poem. Dark Rosaleen. Cathleen ni Houlihan. The nation as woman; the woman as national muse.

The more I looked at it, the more it seemed to me that in relation
to the idea of a nation, many, if not most, Irish male poets had taken
the soft option. The irony was that few Irish poets were national-
ists. By and large, they had eschewed the fervor and crudity of that
ideal. But long after they had rejected the politics of Irish nationalism, they continued to deploy the emblems and enchantments of
its culture. It was the culture, not the politics, which informed Irish
poetry: not the harsh awakenings, but the old dreams.

In all of this I did not blame nationalism. Nationalism seemed
to me inevitable in the Irish context: a necessary hallucination
within Joyce's nightmare of history. I did blame Irish poets. Long

after it was necessary, Irish poetry had continued to trade in the exhausted fictions of the nation; had allowed those fictions to edit ideas of womanhood and modes of remembrance. Some of the poetry produced by such simplifications was, of course, difficult to argue with. It was difficult to deny that something was gained by poems which used the imagery and emblem of the national muse. Something was gained, certainly; but only at an aesthetic level. What was lost occurred at the deepest, most ethical level; and what was lost was what I valued. Not just the details of a past. Not just the hungers, the angers. These, however terrible, remain local. But the truth these details witness—human truths of survival and humiliation—these also were suppressed along with the details. Gone was the suggestion of any complicated human suffering. Instead, you had the hollow victories, the passive images, the rhyming queens.

I knew that the women of the Irish past were defeated. I knew it instinctively long before the Achill woman pointed down the hill to the Keel shoreline. What I objected to was that Irish poetry should defeat them twice.

"I have not written day after day," said Camus, "because I desire the world to be covered with Greek statues and master-pieces. The man who has such a desire does exist in me. But I have written so much because I cannot keep from being drawn towards everyday life, towards those, whoever they may be, who are hu-miliated. They need to hope and, if all keep silent, they will be forever deprived of hope and we with them."

This essay originates in some part from my own need to locate myself in a powerful literary tradition in which until then, or so it seemed to me, I had been an element of design rather than an agent of change. But even as a young poet, and certainly by the time my work confronted me with some of these questions, I had already had a vivid, human witness of the stresses which a national lit-erature can impose on a poet. I had already seen the damage it could do.

I remember the Dublin of the sixties almost more vividly than the city that usurped it. I remember its grace and emptiness and the old hotels with their chintzes and Sheffield trays. In one of these I had tea with Padraic Colum. I find it hard to be exact about the year; somewhere around the mid-sixties. But I have no difficulty at all about the season. It was winter. We sat on a sofa by the window overlooking the street. The lamps were on and a fine rain was being glamourized as it fell past their cowls.

Colum was then in his eighties. He had come from his native Longford in the early years of this century to a Dublin fermenting with political and literary change. Yeats admired his 1913 volume of poetry, *Wild Earth*. He felt the Ireland Colum proposed fit neatly into his own idea. "It is unbeautiful Ireland," Yeats wrote. "He will contrast finely with our Western dialect-makers."

In old photographs Colum looks the part: curly-headed, dark, winsome. In every way he was a godsend to the Irish Revival. No one would actually have used the term "peasant poet." But then no one would have needed to. Such things were understood.

The devil they say casts no shadow. But that folk image applies to more than evil. There are writers in every country who begin in the morning of promise but by the evening, mysteriously, have cast no shadow and left no mark. Colum is one of them. For some reason, although he was eminently placed to deal with the energies of his own culture, he failed to do so. His musical, tender, hopeful imagination glanced off the barbaric griefs of the nineteenth century. It is no good fudging the issue. Very few of his poems now look persuasive on the page. All that heritage which should have been his—rage robbed of language, suffering denied its dignity—somehow eluded him. When he met it at all, it was with a borrowed sophistication.

Now in old age he struggled for a living. He transited stoically between Dublin and New York giving readings, writing articles. He remained open and approachable. No doubt for this reason, I asked him what he really thought of Yeats. He paused for a moment. His voice had a distinctive, treble resonance. When he answered it was high and emphatic. "Yeats hurt me," he said. "He expected too much of me."

I have never been quite sure what Colum meant. What I understand by his words may be different from their intent. But I see his relation with the Irish Revival as governed by corrupt laws of supply and demand. He could only be tolerated if he read the signals right and acquiesced in his role as a peasant poet. He did not and he could not. To be an accomplice in such a distortion required a calculation he never possessed. But the fact that he was screen-tested for it suggests how relentless the idea of Irishness in Irish poetry has been.

Colum exemplified something else to me. Here also was a poet who had been asked to make the journey, in one working lifetime, from being the object of Irish poems to being their author. He, too, as an image, had been unacceptably simplified in all those poems about the land and the tenantry. So that—if he was to realize his identity—not only must he move from image to image-maker, he must also undo the simplifications of the first by his force and command of the second. I suspect he found the imaginative stresses of that transit beyond his comprehension, let alone his strength. And so something terrible happened to him. He wrote Irish poetry as if he were still the object of it. He wrote with the passivity and simplification of his own reflection looking back at him from poems, plays, and novels in which the so-called Irish peasant was son of the earth, a cipher of the national cause.

He had the worst of both worlds.

Like Colum, Francis Ledwidge was born at the sharp end of history. An Irish poet who fought as a British soldier, a writer in a radical situation who used a conservative idiom to support it— Ledwidge's short life was full of contradiction. He was in his early twenties when he died in World War I.

Despite his own marginal and pressured position, Ledwidge used the conventional language of romantic nationalism. Not always; perhaps not often. But his poem on the death of the leaders of the Easter Rising, "The Blackbirds," is a case in point. It is, in a small way, a celebrated poem and I have certainly not chosen it because it represents careless or shoddy work. Far from it. It is a skillful poem, adroit and quick in its rhythms, with an underlying sweetness of tone. For all that, it provides an example of a gifted poet who did not resist the contemporary orthodoxy. Perhaps he might have had he lived longer and learned more. As it was, Ledwidge surrendered easily to the idioms of the Irish Revival. This in turn meant that he could avail himself of a number of approved stereotypes and, chief among them, the easy blend of feminine and national. Even here he could exercise a choice although, it must be said, a limited one. He could have had the young Queen or the old mother. As it happened, he chose the poor old woman. But we are in no doubt what he means:

The Blackbirds

I heard the Poor Old Woman say
"At break of day the fowler came
And took my blackbirds from their song
Who loved me well through shame and blame.

No more from lovely distances
Their songs shall bless me mile from mile,
Nor to white Ashbourne call me down
To wear my crown another while.

With bended flowers the angels mark
For the skylark the place they lie.
From there its little family
Shall dip their wings first in the sky.

And when the first surprise of flight
Sweet songs excite, from the far dawn
Shall there come blackbirds, loud with love,
Sweet echoes of the singers gone.

But in the lovely hush of eve
Weeping I grieve the silent bills"
I heard the Poor Old Woman say
In Derry of the little hills.[1]

I am not sure this poem would pass muster now. There are too many sugary phrases—"loud with love" and "shame and blame"—evoking the very worst of Georgian poetry. But Ledwidge was young and the impulse for the poem was historical. The 1916 leaders were dead. He was at a foreign front. The poem takes on an extra resonance if it is read as a concealed elegy for his own loyalties.

What is more interesting is how, in his attempt to make the feminine stand in for the national, he has simplified the woman in the poem almost out of existence. She is in no sense the poor old woman of the colloquial expression. There are no vulnerabilities here, no human complexities. She is a Poor Old Woman in capital letters. A mouthpiece. A sign.

Therefore the poem divides into two parts: one vital, one inert. The subject of the poem appears to be the woman. But appearances deceive. She is merely the object, the pretext. The real subject is the blackbirds. They are the animated substance of the piece. They call from "lovely distances"; their "sweet songs" "excite" and "bless." Whatever imaginative power the lyric has, it comes from these birds. Like all effective images, the blackbirds have a life outside the poem. They take their literal shape from the birds we know and to these they return an emblematic force. They continue to be vital once the poem is over.

The woman, on the other hand, is a diagram. By the time the poem is over, she has become a dehumanized ornament. When her speaking part finishes she goes out of the piece and out of our memory. At best, she has been the engine of the action; a convenient frame for the proposition.

The question worth asking is whether this fusion of national and feminine, this interpretation of one by the other, is inevitable. It was after all common practice in Irish poetry: Mangan's Dark Rosaleen comes immediately to mind. In fact the custom and the practice reached back, past the songs and simplifications of the nineteenth century, into the Bardic tradition itself. Daniel Corkery referred to this in his analysis of the Aisling convention in *The Hidden Ireland*. "The vision the poet sees," he wrote, "is always the spirit of Ireland as a majestic and radiant maiden."[2]

So many male Irish poets—the later Yeats seems to me a rare exception—have feminized the national and nationalized the feminine that from time to time it has seemed there is no other option. But an Irish writer who turned away from such usages suggests that there was, in fact, another and more subversive choice.

In the opening pages of *Ulysses*, Joyce describes an old woman. She climbs the steps to the Martello tower, darkening its doorway. She is, in fact, the daily milkwoman. but no sooner has she started to pour a quart of milk into Stephen's measure than she begins to shimmer and dissolve into legendary images: "Silk of the kine and poor old woman, names given her in old times. A wandering crone, lowly form of an immortal, serving her conqueror and her gay betrayer, their common cuckquean, a messenger from the secret morning. To serve or to upbraid, whether he could not tell; but scorned to beg her favor."

The same phrase as Ledwidge uses—"poor old woman"—is included here. But whereas Ledwidge used it with a straight face, Joyce dazzles it with irony. By reference and inference, he shows himself to be intent on breaking the traditional association of Ireland with ideas of womanhood and tragic motherhood. After all, these simplifications are part and parcel of what he, Joyce, has painfully rejected. They are some of the reasons he is in exile from the mythos of his own country. Now by cunning inflations, by disproportions of language, he takes his revenge. He holds at a glittering, manageable distance a whole tendency in national thought and expression; and dismisses it. But then Joyce is a poetic moralist. Much of *Ulysses*, after all, is invested in Daedelus's search for the ethical shadow of his own aesthetic longings. He has a difficult journey ahead of him. And Joyce has no intention of letting him be waylaid, so early in the book, by the very self-deceptions he has created him to resolve.

It is easy, and intellectually seductive, for a woman artist to walk away from the idea of a nation. There has been, and there must continue to be, a great deal of debate about the energies and myths women writers should bring with them into a new age. Start again, has been the cry of some of the best feminist poets. Wipe clean the slate, start afresh. It is a potent idea: to begin in a new world, clearing the desert as it were, making it blossom; even making the rain.

In any new dispensation the idea of a nation must seem an expendable construct. After all, it has never admitted of women. Its flags and songs and battle cries, even its poetry, as I've suggested, make use of feminine imagery. But that is all. The true voice and vision of women are routinely excluded.

Then why did I not walk away? Simply because I was not free to. For all my quarrels with the concept, and no doubt partly because of them, I needed to find and repossess that idea at some level of repose. Like the swimmer in Adrienne Rich's poem "Diving into the Wreck," I needed to find out "the damage that was done and the treasures that prevail." I knew the idea was flawed. But if it was flawed, it was also one of the vital human constructs of a place in which, like Leopold Bloom, I was born. More importantly, as a friend and feminist scholar said to me, we ourselves are constructed by the construct. I might be the author of my poems; I was not the author of my past. However crude the diagram, the idea of a nation remained the rough graphic of an ordeal. In some subterranean way I felt myself to be part of that ordeal; its fragmentations extended into mine.

"I am invisible," begins the prologue of Ralph Ellison's novel *The Invisible Man*. "I am invisible, understand, because people refuse to see me. Like the bodyless heads you see sometimes in circus shows it is as though I have been surrounded by mirrors of hard, distorting glass. When they approach me they see only their surroundings, themselves, or figments of their own imagination—indeed everything and anything except me."[3]

In an important sense, Ellison's words applied to the sort of Irish poem which availed of that old, potent blurring of feminine and national. In such poems, the real woman behind the image was not only not explored, she was never even seen. It was a subtle mechanism; subtle and corrupt. And it was linked, I believed, to a wider sequence of things not seen.

A society, a nation, a literary heritage is always in danger of making up its communicable heritage from its visible elements. Women, as it happens, are not especially visible in Ireland. This came to me early and with personal force. I realized when I published a poem that what was seen of me, what drew approval, if it was forthcoming at all, was the poet. The woman, by and large, was invisible. It was an unsettling discovery. Yet I came to believe that my invisibility as a woman was a disguised grace. It had the power to draw me, I sensed, towards realities like the Achill woman. It made clear to me that what she and I shared, apart from those fragile moments of talk, was the danger of being edited out of our own literature by conventional tribalisms.

Marginality within a tradition, however painful, confers certain advantages. It allows the writer clear eyes and a quick critical sense. Above all, the years of marginality suggest to such a writer—and I am speaking of myself now—the real potential of subversion. I wanted to relocate myself within the Irish poetic tradition. I felt the need to do so. I thought of myself as an Irish poet, although I was fairly sure it was not a category that readily suggested itself in connection with my work. A woman poet is rarely regarded as an automatic part of a national poetic tradition; and for the reasons I have already stated. She is too deeply woven into the passive texture of that tradition, too intimate a part of its imagery, to be allowed her freedom. She may know, as an artist, that she is now the maker of the poems and not merely the subject of them. The critique is slow to catch up. There has been a growing tendency in the last few years for academics and critics in this country to discuss women's poetry as a subculture, to keep it quarantined from the main body of poetry. I thought it vital that women poets such as myself should establish a discourse with the idea of the nation. I felt sure that the most effective way to do this was by subverting the previous terms of that discourse. Rather than accept the nation as it appears in Irish poetry, with its queen and muses, I felt the time had come to rework those images by exploring the emblematic relation between my own feminine experience and a national past.

The truths of womanhood and the defeats of a nation? An improbable intersection? At first sight perhaps. Yet the idea of it opened doors in my mind which had hitherto been closed fast. I began to think there was indeed a connection; that my womanhood and my nationhood were meshed and linked at some root. It was not just that I had a womanly feeling for those women who waited with handcarts, went into the sour stomachs of ships, and even—according to terrible legend—eyed their baby's haunches speculatively in the hungers of the 1840s. It was more than that. I was excited by the idea that if there really was an emblematic relation between the defeats of womanhood and the suffering of a nation, I need only prove the first in order to reveal the second. If so, then Irishness and womanhood, those tormenting fragments of my youth, could at last stand in for one another. Out of a painful apprenticeship and an ethical dusk, the laws of metaphor beckoned me.

I was not alone. "Where women write strongly as women," said Alicia Ostriker in her seminal book *Stealing the Language*, "it is clear their intention is to subvert the life and literature they inherit."[4] This was not only true of contemporary women poets. In the terrible years between 1935 and 1940, the Russian poet Anna Akhmatova composed "The Requiem." It was written for her only son, Lev Gumilev, who at the start of the Stalinist Terror had been arrested, released, rearrested. Then, like so many others, he disappeared into the silence of a Leningrad prison. For days, months, years Akhmatova queued outside. The "Epilogue to the Requiem" refers to that experience. What is compelling and instructive is the connection it makes between her womanhood and her sense of a nation as a community of grief. The country she wishes to belong to, to be commemorated by, is the one revealed to her by her suffering:

> And if ever in this country they should want
> To build me a monument
>
> I consent to that honor
> But only on condition that they
>
> Erect it not on the seashore where I was born:
> My last links with that were broken long ago,
> Nor by the stump in the Royal Gardens
> Where an inconsolable young shade is seeking me
>
> But here, where I stood for three hundred hours
> And where they never, ever opened the doors for me
>
> Lest in blessed death I should ever forget
> The grinding scream of the Black Marias,
>
> The hideous clanging gate, the old
> Woman wailing like a wounded beast.[5]

I am concerned that in the process of summarizing this argument, it may take on a false symmetry. I have, after all, been describing ideas and impressions as if they were events. I have been proposing thoughts and perceptions in a way they did not and could not occur. I have given hard shapes and definite outlines to feelings which were far more hesitant.

The reality was different. Exact definitions do not happen in the real life of a poet; and certainly not in mine. I have written here about the need to repossess the idea of a nation. But there was nothing assured or automatic about it. "It is not in the darkness of belief that I desire you," says Richard Rowan at the end of Joyce's *Exiles*, "but in restless, living, wounding doubt." I had the additional doubts of a writer who knows that a great deal of their literary tradition has been made up in ignorance of their very existence; that its momentum has been predicated on simplifications of their complexity. Yet I still wished to enter that tradition; although I knew my angle of entry must be oblique. None of it was easy. I reached tentative havens after figurative storms. I came to understand what Mallarmé meant when he wrote: "Each newly acquired truth was born only at the expense of an impression that flamed up and then burned itself out, so that its particular darkness could not be isolated."

My particular darkness as an Irish poet has been the subject of this piece. But there were checks and balances. I was, as I have said, a woman in a literary tradition which simplified women. I was also a poet lacking the precedent and example of previous Irish women poets. These were the givens of my working life. But if these circumstances displaced my sense of relation to the Irish past in Irish poetry, they also forced me into a perception of the advantages of being able to move, with almost surreal inevitability, from being within the poem to being its maker. A hundred years ago I might have been a motif in a poem. Now I could have a complex self within my own poem. Part of that process entailed being a privileged witness to forces of reaction in Irish poetry.

Some of these I have named. The tendency to fuse the national and the feminine, to make the image of the woman the pretext of a romantic nationalism—these have been the weaknesses in Irish poetry. As a young poet, these simplifications isolated and estranged me. They also made it clearer to me that my own discourse must be subversive . In other words, that I must be vigilant to write of my own womanhood—whether it was revealed to me in the shape of a child or a woman from Achill—in such a way that I never colluded with the simplified images of women in Irish poetry.

When I was young all this was comfortless. I took to heart the responsibility of making my own critique, even if for years it consisted of little more than accusing Irish poetry in my own mind of deficient ethics. Even now I make no apology for such a critique. I believe it is still necessary. Those simplified women, those conventional reflexes and reflexive feminizations of the national experience; those static, passive, ornamental figures do no credit to a poetic tradition which has been, in other respects, radical and innovative, capable of both latitude and compassion.

But there is more to it. As a young poet I would not have felt so threatened and estranged if the issue had merely been the demands a national program makes on a country's poetry. The real issue went deeper. When I read those simplifications of women I felt there was an underlying fault in Irish poetry; almost a geological weakness. All good poetry depends on an ethical relation between imagination and image. Images are not ornaments; they are truths. When I read about Cathleen ni Houlihan or the Old Woman of the Roads or Dark Rosaleen, I felt that a necessary ethical relation was in danger of being violated over and over again; that a merely ornamental relation between imagination and image was being handed on from poet to poet, from generation to generation; was becoming orthodox poetic practice. It was the violation, even more than the simplification, which alienated me.

No poetic imagination can afford to regard an image as a temporary aesthetic maneuver. Once the image is distorted the truth is demeaned. That was the heart of it all as far as I was concerned. In availing themselves of the old convention, in using and reusing women as icons and figments, Irish poets were not just dealing with emblems. They were also evading the real women of an actual past: women whose silence their poetry should have broken. They ran the risk of turning a terrible witness into an empty decoration. One of the ironic purposes of my argument has been to point out that those emblems are no longer silent. They have acquired voices. They have turned from poems to poets.

Writers, if they are wise, do not make their home in any comfort within a national tradition. However vigilant the writer, however enlightened the climate, the dangers persist. So too do the obligations. There is a recurring temptation for any nation, and for any writer who operates within its field of force, to make an ornament of the past; to turn the losses to victories and to restate humiliations as triumphs. In every age language holds out narcosis and amnesia for this purpose. But such triumphs in the end are unsustaining and may, in fact, be corrupt.

If a poet does not tell the truth about time, his or her work will not survive it. Past or present, there is a human dimension to time, human voices within it and human griefs ordained by it. Our present will become the past of other men and women. We depend on them to remember it with the complexity with which it was suffered. As others, once, depended on us.

NOTES

This essay first appeared in *American Poetry Review,* VOL. 19, NO. 2 (March/April 1990). It is reprinted here with the permission of the author.

1. Francis Ledwidge, *The Complete Poems* (London: H. Jenkins, Ltd., 1944), p. 136.

2. Daniel Corkery, *The Hidden Island* (Eire: Gill and Macmillan, 1983).

3. Ralph Ellison, *Invisible Man* (New York: Random House, 1952), p. 3.

4. Alicia Ostriker, *Stealing the Language: The Emergence of Women's Poetry in America* (Boston: Beacon Press, 1986).

5. Anna Akhmatova, "Epilogue to Requiem: II," *Requiem and Poem without a Hero,* trans. D. M. Thames (Athens: Ohio U. Press, 1976), p. 32.

LASTING THE NIGHT

Amy Clampitt

By the time I graduated from high school I had discovered the poems of Edna St. Vincent Millay, then very much in fashion. The spring of 1937 is a long time ago, and it may be that I only imagine what I seem to recall—namely, aspiring to what the first of her Figs from Thistles called "burning at both ends." Oh yes, I was going to be a Writer, but that was no more than ancillary. To put it another way, it meant getting out—out of the rural scene where my own psychic halts and festinations, my lunges toward self-definition, were all egregiously out of sync.

Looking back, I'm not sure how much gender had to do with this quasi-paralysis. My parents had been similarly lacking in assurance; but I have a sense that it was my father, as head of the household, on whom the burden of anxiety chiefly fell. *His* father had left a poignant record, whose importance to me can scarcely be exaggerated, of anxiety amounting almost to terror. It may be that my mother and my grandmothers suffered no less; but if so, they set down no such record. For my mother there was the recourse of tears, which made everybody feel guilty, whereas for the men in my family, whatever feeling was openly expressed took the form of anger. Setting things down could make a difference, as I seem to have known from an early age; but the legacy of self-doubt remained.

Why were we all so unsure of ourselves, so fearful of exposure, so open to ridicule, to throttling worry about what other people might think or say? It wasn't simply money, though we were pinched for it. As I would learn much later, such anxieties had been known to Virginia Woolf; and it was she, through the language of *The Waves*, who seemed to be speaking to and for an isolation so precarious that I, as a college sophomore, hadn't dared suppose it could be the plight of anyone else. Her being a novelist, so called, rather than a poet, had perhaps something to do with the kind of writer I now intended to be.

Back in high school, I'd written a number of sonnets—Shakespeare, not Millay, being the real exemplar, so far as I remember. But in those days (however improbable it might seem, given the ever-dwindling margin of concern with what is wistfully called "the examined life" as a matter of public discourse), the notion of becoming a poet was more fraught with ridicule than now. The sources of this paradox are for cultural historians to mull over. One effect of the sixties was a general blurring of the old stereotypes, that of the poet among them. I seem to remember, from Ernie Kovacs' long-gone gallery of losers, one Percy something—was it Silvertonsils? He was, at any rate, unmistakably, effeminately, The Poet. Nowadays, live poets from time to time make an appearance on television—marginally but without (so far as I know) being lampooned. Men once sneered at Culture because they felt in some way threatened by it, in much the same way (I believe) that they felt threatened by women. The way men feel threatened by women has changed; as for the feminine aspect associated with Higher Things, the sneer would seem to have been replaced by indifference. In my own reluctance to assume the label of poet(ess), gender must thus have been a factor, but one so pervasive that I hardly knew how to think about it.

Others did, certainly: the most vivid member of the campus literary elite (who would go on to write prose, not verse) addressed herself, in a poem I still remember, to Milton's "He for God only, she for God in him"—though in a tone more adoring of a particular male than bitter concerning the female condition.

Having geared myself toward prose, I never considered taking a course in verse writing. One had been offered, taught by a woman who never, if I remember correctly, got past the rank of assistant professor. (The department included two other women; all three were single, and their position on campus and beyond was, accordingly, the more anomalous.) After college, I was not to attempt anything in verse for something like fifteen years. As for that alluring First Fig, I can only say that lasting the night, and still more the feat of getting through the day, had given me pause.

During those years, sporadically, I tried my hand at fiction. The reluctant and gradual conclusion that I must after all be, if anything, a poet, coincided more or less with the upheavals of the sixties. The exhilaration of those upheavals was liberating for me, bringing me as near as I've ever come to the equivalent of "burning at both ends." The anxiety that had kept me throttled now lifted sufficiently to reveal a new world of possibility. I am simplifying, I suppose; but as though for the first time, I felt free to be a poet. It was even, in the lingo of the moment, a neat thing to be.

I was reading Sylvia Plath in those days, and at the same time I was aware of scathings from the blast furnace of radical feminism. My response to both was initially one of resistance: a poem entitled "After Reading Sylvia Plath" began, if I remember right, by saying, "No, no, I do not want it," and one called "Models" ended with an appalled repudiation of what I had heard at one high-pitched gathering, where women were "afraid of not agreeing, it will mean they are not brave." If I did pick up, perhaps, a bit of swagger, a change of manner, from what was being resisted, it was little more that that. Emily Dickinson had not yet spoken to me, nor had Marianne Moore; the few anthologized pieces I knew would remain impenetrable for a while longer. The day would come when, awakened to the inclusiveness and particularity of Marianne Moore's work, I would discover in it a new way of proceeding. Even then, the poets whose longtime influence chiefly obtained were Keats and Hopkins, Milton and Donne. No wonder, then, that an offering to the editors of *Aphra* came back with the complaint, "We don't hear *your* voice." From other periodicals, years of silence—broken finally, as it happens, by an editor who happened to be male.

Do I feel left out? From the perspective of one who has been helped more by men than by women, the question has a ring of almost comic irrelevance—the one reasonable answer being, Of course, who doesn't? My own case (as one critic, a woman, a bit crossly called it) may itself be irrelevant, a mere anomaly. Or is it perhaps that to be anomalous is finally inseparable from what makes a poet, of either sex?

RECLAIMING THE OH

Martha Collins

Our tongue is the mother tongue: we learn it from our mothers. At least we did when I was a child: mothers were the bedtime storytellers, after-school listeners. Father-activities were mostly physical: rough-housing, piggyback; talk was left to Mom.

Mine began with basics. Oh, she said; Oh, I said. Ah, she said; Ah, I said. Or so I'm told. Vowel play. Assonance. Then rhyme: Ah! La!

School was women. Mrs. Healey, gypsy-scarved and gypsy-earringed, asking for stories from second graders, setting my mother straight: "Your daughter isn't telling lies; she just has an imagination." And Miss Smith, daughter of Adam, giving her third-grade pupils the names of rocks, animals, plants.

Poems began to make occasional appearances in the elementary curriculum. Shut my eyes and the first I remember is Christina Rossetti: "Who has seen the wind? / Neither I nor you." Then Emily Dickinson: "I'm nobody! Who are you?" Women poets; poems about invisibility.

But where, in those early years, was Daddy? Where was the phallocentric language we hear so much about these days? This much needs to be said: we all, men included, learn it first from women—or we did, in those days before men started helping with the children. Which isn't to say that patriarchal language wasn't ready to rush in, from the moment we opened our books: history books, math books (how many men working how many hours?), reading books with stories about boys. The only reader story I remember is one about boy-and-girl twins: the boy, star of the team, is sick; the girl, disguised as her brother, saves the day with a home run.

I remember more from later years, when "literature" replaced readers, an event marked by the new importance given to authors' names. Those, too, were mostly male—except, in high school, for Dickinson and George Eliot; except, in college, for those and the Brontës and Woolf. Only one woman poet, and it wasn't, then, Dickinson who drew me; what turned me from law school (could I be Perry Mason?) were one novel and one poem, both written by men. Henry James' *Portrait of a Lady* came first: I loved the writing, the richness of it, but I loved the lady too, the richness of *her*. Then Wallace Stevens' "Sunday Morning," answering unvoiced conflicts with unvoiced longings, not to mention that I'd discovered Poetry. But now I see something more: there's a woman again, in a man's hands, and maybe in dialogue with him (is that her voice, or his?), but at least it's her mind.

It was, then, a male tradition that drew me to literature; but the reading list was edited, sometimes favoring works that featured women, always avoiding the truly troublesome ones. Thus, I suspect, women readers confronting a primarily male tradition have often made up their own version of it, as well as their own version of individual writers (skip the part about Eve). And I suspect that women have, in this way, influenced the shape of that tradition: would Jane Austen—or even Henry James—be quite so alive and well without our votes?

And what of women writers? Slow in becoming one myself, I went off to graduate school and did a dissertation on James, its centerpiece the essay on Isabel Archer I'd been reworking since undergraduate days. But I'd gone, by a fluke, to the University of Iowa, and along the way happened into a workshop course where Catherine B. Davis, a somewhat older student who was already an accomplished poet, gave a wonderful lecture on poetic diction one day. Only now do I realize that it was the first class I'd heard a woman teach since I was in high school.

At a distance, Catherine B. Davis became my mentor. Closer to the desk where I kept the journal in which notes were occasionally becoming lines, I began to pursue women writers. I read Woolf straight through, the way I'd read James; Dickinson's *Collected Poems* took their place beside Stevens'. Later, after I'd discovered Williams, I read all of Denise Levertov, over and over; then, after I'd taken in all Theodore Roethke had to offer, I turned to his mentor, Louise Bogan. That Bogan's poems were difficult was part of the attraction: under the skillful surface was something I somehow sensed I needed, if I was myself to write.

Thus, like many women of my generation, I began to learn from female voices for the first time since childhood, recovering what I'd repressed or suppressed or maybe just forgotten. For a year or so I read almost nothing but books by and about women. The aim, for me, was clearly balance: I'd been given the male writers; now I was finding the women, often as direct "counters" to the men.

This balancing act is not, I think, uncommon. For years, Emily Dickinson was seen as part of the male tradition (the only woman, in fact, in the boys-only American literature club), and certainly one can't read her without an intense awareness of the patriarchal texts behind her, the Bible most emphatically among them. But recent critics have shown us that Dickinson was also influenced by women writers: Elizabeth Barrett Browning, for one, but also the popular and largely forgotten women poets of nineteenth-century America. A similar balance can be found in Elizabeth Bishop: David Kalstone's *Becoming a Poet* traces the importance of first Marianne Moore, then Robert Lowell in Bishop's development.

The order of influence Kalstone finds in Bishop mirrors, in another area, the developmental shift from mother to father traced by Freud and others, which the culture of my youth prescribed as the norm for all women. Born into a decidedly prefeminist age, we broke our female ties early; growing up meant growing into a world of male authority, and active participation in that world—as opposed to marriage to it—meant putting on our brothers' uniforms and playing ball with them. That one could define achievement in female terms, or at any rate with female models, was the welcome news of my early adulthood; for some of us it was introductory to a much deeper awareness of female roots. Unavailable as model of achievement—or, if we happened to be heterosexual, as love-object—our first love returned to some of us with an almost overwhelming force. One of course needn't delve so deeply to explain our dual heritage: male literary dominance has made our literary as well as our cultural position not altogether dissimilar to the African-American "double-consciousness" described by Du Bois. But I suspect that the basis of our dual allegiance is as deeply psychological as it is broadly social.

Which is not to say that balancing two traditions is an easy matter, especially in a culture that dichotomizes as much as ours does. We may think of dichotomizing as a particularly male business, but pressure has come from the other side too: if writing has traditionally been seen as phallic (oh that pen!), some feminist theorists have posited and promoted a shift to another kind of voicing; thus Luce Irigary, "when our lips speak to each other." It probably is true that ultimate balance can occur only if some women speak primarily to and of one another, at least for awhile; it's difficult not to be grateful for the period in which Adrienne Rich, dreaming of a common language, spoke only "lips to lips."

But the mouth, where it all begins, is remarkably androgynous, tongue and lips working together, and women may, for developmental and other reasons, be the more androgynous of the sexes. As men begin to put in more real time at bedtime, and women are heard and read in colleges as well as elementary schools, differences between experiences and traditions may diminish. For the time being, it may be part of the woman writer's business to do some reclaiming and balancing.

For me, at least, one aim of writing poetry, however unrealizable, is a reclamation of all the language I have known. It's not a matter of discovering a new woman's language, but rather of retrieving an old one—one that includes not only the voicings of infancy, but also the vocabulary and syntax given by mothers and women teachers. That the acquisition of this language both depended on and reinforced physical and emotional ties is one source of its enduring strength: if we were fortunate in our mothers, we learned those first words and sentences in the same moments that, arms around us, we were learning what it meant to be connected to another human being.

That men learned language in the same way, from the same women, is a well-kept secret. But the repressed is never altogether absent: the mother turns up as muse, and poetry, with its ahs and las, its embrace of physical and emotional as well as intellectual truth, is perhaps the place where even the most patriarchal language has continued to reveal its origins. Thus, I suspect, my attraction to poems in the first place. If it were merely a matter of tradition, as Eliot defines it (the "whole of the literature of Europe" and so forth), the territory would be too small. The challenge and pleasure is to include and make visible what was obscured: not to accept old restrictions, not to substitute new ones, but to retrieve, balance, relate, and unite, ohs and odes, ahs and amens informing and speaking to one other.

FIGURES IN THE LOOKING-GLASS: TRADITION, GENDER BIAS, AND THE TALENTED WOMAN

Madeline DeFrees

> *Mirror, mirror on the wall,* *,llaw eht no rorrim ,rorriM*
> *Who's the most traditional?* *?lanigiro tsom eht s'ohW*

"Writing is not in the least an easy art," Virginia Woolf notes in her diary,[1] and here to make it harder than it already is is "Tradition and the Individual Talent," with its lavish prescriptions for reading the whole of English literature, the major European writers, and the early Greek and Latin classics—all before age twenty-five. And during one's idle moments, it would be useful to learn several foreign languages. All this to achieve the "historical sense," which Eliot considers "nearly indispensable to anyone who would continue beyond *his* twenty-fifth year" (my emphasis). Fortunately, Eliot has left a small escape hatch through the gaps in the possessive pronoun, else I should have to shut up shop before I begin. I was twenty-nine when I received the B.A. in English literature after twelve years of patchwork study, and at seventy-two I have yet to read Edmund Spenser and—yes—William Blake. I don't say this to boast, but merely to signal a not-untypical record for women of my generation whose lives were governed by sets of priorities different from those of men. Besides, some of us were deterred by the questionable enthusiasms of male colleagues like the young man who devoted roughly equal time to experimenting with LSD and teaching William Blake. He used to come into my office regularly, eyes glittering like the Ancient Mariner's, and repeat the highlights of what I guessed to be that day's lecture, liberally sprinkled with quotations from his favorite poet: "Better to strangle an infant in the cradle than to nurture a single unacted desire." That may not be verbatim, but the gist is accurate. Furthermore, one of his students, asking to enroll in my poetry workshop, proposed bringing in "a Blakean epic" as his first submission. I could have been more tactful in my response (it was a workshop in the lyric, we did not have a week to spend on one person's work, etc.), but I spoke too soon and too bluntly. He signed up for Richard Hugo's course, where, if I know anything about Dick, he was not allowed to unreel his masterpiece. But Dick would have known how to say no without bruising the student's ego.

In the halcyon days before Mount Helicon erupted and permanently altered the literary landscape, Hugo used to explain men's dominance of the poetic tradition in this way: *Men have weaker egos and stronger personalities.* At first glance, this statement appears to contradict Eliot's contention that "The progress of an artist is a continual extinction of personality." On closer examination, however, Hugo seems to be in essential agreement with Eliot on this point. Eliot uses "personality" in two distinct ways, as Northrop Frye points out: 1) in its ordinary sense; and 2) to designate the creative personality.[2] Whatever Hugo may have had in mind in the pronouncement just quoted, he makes it clear elsewhere that he sometimes uses *personality* to denote *persona*—or, in Yeats's glossary, *mask.* Hugo's favorite term for the creative personality is *stance,* as he makes clear in an interview with Thomas Gardner:

> Q. In "Statements of Faith" you say that "Certain feelings lead to certain stances in the poem. If the feelings are strong enough the stances may be overstances, or poses." Is stance also a way of initiating poems?
>
> A. When I talk about stance I'm talking about becoming the kind of person necessary to use the language you're using. In "Leda and the Swan" Yeats would have had to be an uncompromising person to write that first line: "A sudden blow; the great wings beating still. . . ." You see, he would have had to be there instantly on stage in the middle of the act because he starts the poem not with Zeus getting an erection but in the middle of rape. That's a stance: there's a kind of person you have to be to start a poem. Usually I find if I start out too loudly, that if I go back and take a

softer beginning, I'm sometimes able to get the poems where I wasn't able to with the other opening.

Later in the same interview, we encounter:

Q. Some of your poems take that tough opening then change in the middle.

A. Yes, that's right: Humphrey Bogart going in and Leslie Howard coming out, which is typical of me. I've always wanted to be a tough guy and I never was, of course.

When Gardner asks whether Hugo sees any difference between autobiography and a lyric poem, Hugo answers that the autobiography is more inclusive. The lyric, on the other hand, tends "to deliberately create things." He notes that memory may alter the content of autobiography and continues:

... Auden says when we look in the mirror we never see ourselves because we always compose our face into the face we want to see, before we look. I believe that memory does that too: it creates the situation into one where you fit in, one way or another. So, it's always a kind of lie, but not a deliberate lie. In a poem, you'll fictionalize something just to see where the possibilities in the language take you.[3]

To compose one's face into the face one wants to see in the mirror is another form of stance: strength of personality compensating for a weak ego. If Hugo actually seemed to believe that men dominated the tradition because they wrote more and better, it may be that he extrapolated his personal experience into a universal and assigned the ego-personality theory as cause. But as we now know, other factors, cultural and historic, conspired to keep women from both the exercise and the public acceptance of their literary talent.

Later, there will be occasion to return to the mirror, but for now let me report another of Hugo's favorite routines: *Men are better poets because the Muse is a woman.* At one public gathering, when my ego was weak and my personality somewhat stronger, I answered with more edge than I care to confess: "Speak for yourself, Dick. Your Muse may be a woman, but. . . ." As with so much else, time has levelled the playing field and widened the spectrum of sexual preference to such a degree as to render both Hugo's assertion and my rejoinder largely irrelevant.

It's a curious concept, Eliot's vision of the literary tradition as a vast game of musical chairs in which the ghosts of writers past (male) and their living counterparts (male) move round and round an imaginary center, in constantly shifting relation, each hoping not to be the one unseated when the music winds down. How many women would think of themselves and their literary niches in such terms? For Eliot *is* thinking of his particular rung on the literary ladder, despite protestations of humility, admonitions to self-sacrifice, and caveats against the self-important ego. Elsewhere he tells us that a poet's critical views are not to be trusted; that they must always be considered in relation to the poems he writes, because the poet is more advocate than judge and his knowledge is likely to be incomplete, owing to a habit of concentrating on one or two figures—the very practice he warns against in "Tradition and the Individual Talent."[4] Nor does he feel obligated to account for his inconsistencies. Like Whitman, he says in effect:

> Do I contradict myself?
> Very well then I contradict myself.
> (I am large, I contain multitudes.)
> > "Song of Myself," stanza 51

Being small and less capacious, in spite of having given birth to Whitman, Eliot, and every other poet, Woman must be content with patience under attack and with more modest pretensions, illustrated by this entry from Virginia Woolf's diary:

> . . . In today's *Lit. Sup.*, they advertise Men without Art, by Wyndham Lewis: chapters on Eliot, Faulkner, Hemingway, Virginia Woolf. . . Now I know by instinct that this is an attack; that I am publicly demolished; nothing is left of me in Oxford and Cambridge and places where the young read Wyndham Lewis. My instinct is not to read it. . . . [5]

Then she resumes reading Keats and finds this:

> Praise or blame has but a momentary effect on the man whose love of beauty in the abstract makes him a severe critic of his own

works. . . . This is a mere matter of the moment—I think I shall be among the English poets after my death. . . .

Returning to her own situation, Woolf writes:

> . . . Well: do I think I shall be among the English novelists after my death? I hardly ever think about it. Why then do I shrink from reading W. L.? Why am I sensitive? I think vanity: I dislike the thought of being laughed at. . . perhaps I feel uncertain about my own gifts. . . anyhow I intend to go on writing.[6]

This mixture of confidence and insecurity is what I experience as a woman writer. Sometimes doubt paralyzes me, the voices of Woolf's "visionary censors" become deafening. But at intervals I am almost manic and confidence spills ink all over the page. Ideas come from every direction, and all of them seem wonderful. It is both heartening and enabling to find a woman writer whose landscape consists of these peaks and valleys.

The historical sense Eliot speaks of is largely a male historical sense: it does not, for the most part, reflect women's experience. Instinctively and with growing certainty, talented women have come to recognize that the historical record is biased and incomplete. If they themselves feel the necessity to create poems and stories, paintings and sculptures, music and dance, surely their counterparts in earlier times must have felt this need. Yet growing evidence seems to indicate that the "record" tends to obscure or minimize or reassign some of the best work of women artists. Thus, women have begun to re-examine the "record" with a view to revising and expanding it. They are no longer willing to endorse only those women poets, for example, who conform to the critical preconceptions of men. Thus, the range of possibilities in subject matter and form, in perspective and style, has broadened to include the other half of the human race. If exclusivity is required as a temporary corrective to the imbalance, so be it. The pendulum will return to the center, once a more nearly equal balance is achieved. In a recent essay on the theme of "Gender Equity and Institutional Change," Michele Birch-Conery writes:

> In my doctoral dissertation, I spoke about "homelessness in the language" as a way of creating a metaphor for my deep silence and alienation as a woman writer. For a long time, I had been attempt-

ing to articulate the differences I experienced reading male and female texts. I called the former experience "double reading" which meant reading male texts from the dominant cultural perspectives while, at the same time, "unreading" them, or searching them for what was missing. With female texts, especially those which were overtly feminist, I found myself experiencing cultural identification at last. These reading experiences were thoroughly autobiographical in that I began accessing the realities of my life and consequently, creating texts that expressed them. . . .[7]

In place of the metaphor of home, I should like to substitute the looking-glass, taking a leaf from Virginia Woolf and extending the application to other aspects of the milieu in which the woman writer exercises her art. "Women have served all these centuries as looking-glasses," Woolf writes, "possessing the magic and delicious power of reflecting the figure of man at twice its natural size."[8] In too many instances, the mirror-function is not reciprocal, the woman's lot being to find her figure reduced in the man-mirror. And if, as Woolf contends, "mirrors are essential to all violent and heroic action," if "[t]he looking-glass vision is of supreme importance because it charges the vitality [and] stimulates the nervous system," what hope is there for the woman writer?[9] A child needs mirrors, photographs, and healthy social interaction to develop an enabling self-image. The poet, especially in the beginning, needs similar reflections to arrive at an enabling sense of her individual talent. Four kinds of mirrors play a part: 1) the long Mirror of Tradition ,with its closely linked Mirror of Language; 2) the Role Model Mirror, a temporary aid in the early phase of work; 3) the Mirror of Criticism; and 4) the Virginia Woolf Mirror. No doubt there are others, but these are the looking-glasses that have helped or hindered me in my own work.

The Mirror of Tradition

Tradition and the individual talent: the figure of the poet and the reflection in the mirror. The writer in her context, cultural and historic. Two aspects of a single image to satisfy our deepest need for likeness and difference. For a long time, the mirror of tradition a woman looked into was virtually blank. It resembled the mirror Otto Rank speaks of in *The Double*, in which there is no reflection because someone has stolen away the self or the soul or the life of the person confronting the blank looking-glass.

Under such circumstances, it is easy for a woman to conclude that she is a literary nonentity, that her life as writer counts for nothing. Else why would it leave no impression or, worse still, be considered only as a subcategory? What serious writer fancies being called an authoress or a poetess? What satisfaction attends on being designated (as Virginia Woolf once was) "the ablest of the women writers"? It is, perhaps, this system of separate categories that accounts for the reluctance of certain women to publish in journals exclusively for women. Personally, I've always been willing to go along with "separate but equal" until such times as unisex takes over in literature as it has in clothing and coiffures.

When women were published—often as not without their prior knowledge (as is the case of at least one poem by Emily Dickinson)—it was sometimes considered unseemly to attach their names. Thus Ann Stanford notes in her introduction to *The Women Poets in English:*

> . . . In 1650 Mistress [Anne] Bradstreet's brother-in-law took her poems to London, where they were printed without her knowledge. The little book did not bear her name, but was called *The Tenth Muse Lately Sprung Up in America . . . By a Gentlewoman in those parts*.[10]

It was further thought necessary to explain in the preface that the author had not neglected her household duties but had borrowed time from "sleep and other refreshments." Like many another outdated practice, the anonymity and the rationale were both still in force in the convent I entered in 1936.

I was sixteen when I arrived at the novitiate. I had been scribbling verse since I was eleven, when our seventh grade class was assigned to write a Mother's Day poem. After mine was proclaimed the best, I became a kind of class laureate, generating verse for every occasion. Privately, I read the Untermeyer anthologies and books on versification. When I found an anthologized poem I admired, I looked for a whole book by that poet and I wrote parodies of my favorites—though I wouldn't have called them that, since they were all deadly serious. All this activity issued in publication in the high school literary magazine and in the Oregon

Journal. In Hillsboro, poetic terrain was my exclusive property. At St. Mary's there were a few other contenders, but in the novitiate I was surrounded by versifiers. Something in that rarefied atmosphere inspired pious sentiments in rhyme and harmless formal exercises designed to reinforce and celebrate the Religious life. I knew at once that the difference between me and most of the others was that I would continue: writing poems, Keats and Coleridge and negative capability notwithstanding, was the closest I had come to individuation. Without poems, the center would not hold.

Imagine the shock, then, when Sister Margaret Jean, my favorite history teacher from high school, my ongoing mentor, and my intellectual heroine, casually inquired one day, "Why do you bother writing poems?" She had a way of dropping bombs without warning, but this one caught me completely offguard. I must have showed her a recent poem or burbled on about something I was working on. Did she pose the question because she knew, in her shrewd and truthful way of confronting reality, that a nun couldn't get to first base writing poems? I had already felt some uneasiness on this score myself, as if I were always looking over my shoulder expecting someone in authority to say that I must stop writing, that it meant too much to me. The nun's top priority was holiness, which she must pursue with the same passionate intensity the poet reserved for her art. But Sister Margaret Jean made clear her conviction that it wasn't just nuns, but *women*, who lacked the freedom to write important poems. Society had so circumscribed their minds and imaginations that they didn't stand a chance. History and culture had thrown up walls unlikely to be breached in my lifetime. As a fiction writer, I might have a long chance because there were role models among the nineteenth-century novelists.

The Role Model Mirror

Role models are a kind of mirror in the sense that Virginia Woolf speaks of: a vision to charge the energy and stimulate the nervous system. Like many women of my time and after, I looked for them and was nearly always disappointed, as the mirror filled with genteel three-name lady poets who should have taught refractory children or written advice to the lovelorn. Their didacticism recalled the reams of Longfellow I'd memorized as a child: I wanted none of that. Later, there were Elinor Wylie, whom I preferred to Sara Teasdale; Edna St. Vincent Millay, whose subject matter left me cold; Elizabeth Barrett Browning (I preferred Robert); Christina Rossetti. Finally: Emily Dickinson, Marianne Moore, and Louise Bogan. For some reason, I didn't encounter Elizabeth Bishop until much later, and at first I couldn't relate to her poems—maybe the plain style escaped me. But when I took up her poems again in New England, I couldn't believe that I had been so obtuse.

Through the early years, I kept a running list of negative models: male poets whose egos were too large for my schoolgirl looking-glass. Engraved there were the names of Milton, Matthew Arnold, Wordsworth, and Whitman. Although I may have been too glib in my rejections, I rationalized them by saying that these writers lacked the sense of humor that restores a sense of proportion: they took themselves too seriously. In *Samson Agonistes* I discovered that I was wrong about Milton, though I still think that his ego sometimes gets in the way:

> *Here be tears of perfect moan*
> *Wept for thee on Helicon.*
> "Epitaph on the Marchioness of Winchester"

When Milton uses the Marchioness, who died in childbirth at twenty-three, as a mirror, the lines quoted may be said to violate Eliot's strictures against the self-important ego. The spotlight shifts abruptly from the dead woman to the living poet, else why bring up Helicon at all? The reader surprises Milton center stage weeping "tears of perfect moan," which are clearly crocodile tears, a pretext for showing off his literary prowess. One is tempted to wish that the distance between Milton's art and the event were less absolute.

Inevitably, during my early days in the convent, there were the nun-poets. The inward-turning of institutional life tends to create its own models. I looked for guidance to the two or three poets I knew in the order and the dozen or so nuns of other orders publishing in the Catholic magazines all of us read. I perused the literary nuns with gluttonous haste, looking for strength I seldom found, although there were several competent writers among them. Their Religious names trailed strings of initials identifying their respective orders. My favorite was Sister Maura, a School Sister of Notre Dame, whose range was limited but whose satiric thrusts at such targets as modern advertising spoke to my ironic sense. But what I really needed from these women was the assurance that one could be both poet and nun.

Eventually, Gerard Manley Hopkins won out over Emily Dickinson, chiefly because he was allowed during canonical year and she was not. Our studies during that year were confined to theology and philosophy, but Father Hopkins was a religious poet whose lines could serve as texts to memorize, meditate, and imitate, however imperfectly. I would never recommend either of these poets as models for beginning writers, but they are certainly worth reading and rereading. It took me a long time to pull away from the Hopkins influence, but when I did, I was allowed to join the Catholic Poetry Society of America and begin submitting poems to *Spirit*. I was thirty when I published my first poem there in 1949 and began submitting to other magazines, most of them Catholic. In 1950, when I began teaching at the college level, I had more freedom to read, found other poets whose work helped me, and began to deal with criticism from editors and reviewers as well as poets whom I knew personally.

The Mirror of Criticism

In the passage about visionary censors, Virginia Woolf elaborates:

> If I say this, So-and-so will think me sentimental. If that. . . will think me bourgeois. All books now seem to me surrounded by a circle of invisible censors. Hence their selfconsciousness, their restlessness. It would be worthwhile trying to discover what they are at the moment. Did Wordsworth have them? I doubt it. I read "Ruth" before breakfast. Its stillness, its un-consciousness, its lack of distraction, its concentration and the resulting "beauty" struck me. As if the mind must be allowed to settle undisturbed over the object to secrete the pearl.[11]

In her attempts to deal with these distracting voices, Virginia Woolf developed what she called the "philosophy of anonymity," trying insofar as possible to ignore fashion and the success of her peers and "walk over the marsh saying, I am I: and must follow that furrow, not copy another."[12] Like most of us, she was not always successful, and the costs were often extremely high as she battled headaches, nervous fatigue, and suicidal impulses. Yet she pushed forward in spite of all. Here is a typical entry from her diary:

> *Reviewing* came out last week; and was not let slip into obscurity as I expected. *Lit. Sup.* had a tart and peevish leader; the old tone of voice I know so well—rasped and injured. Then Y. Y. polite but aghast in the N. S. And then my answer—why an answer should always make me dance like a monkey at the Zoo, gibbering it over as I walk, and then re-writing, I don't know. It wasted a day. I suppose it's all pure waste: yet if one's an outsider, be an outsider. Only don't for God's sake attitudinise and take up the striking, the becoming attitude.[13]

A large part of the problem was, of course, that Virginia Woolf was an innovator, an original who refused to do anything but grow and change. To read *A Writer's Diary* or reread the body of her work reminds us how much she contributed to the tradition and to the forging of an environment more conducive to women's work.

The Critical Mirror hasn't been a major problem for me simply because I've had the use of it so seldom. When my first collection, *From the Darkroom*, came out in 1964, I was forty-five. The book was shelved with Religion, omitted from the advertising budget, ignored by reviewers, remaindered before it earned the five-hundred-dollar advance Bobbs-Merrill had paid. Today it is impossible to find, even in the Seattle Public Library—where it was placed among the discards and purchased by an alert male poet. After *Darkroom*, it was fourteen years before Braziller published *When Sky Lets Go*—thanks to Richard Howard. Reviewers tended to latch onto the convent past and come up with predictable stereotypes: like Donne's *Holy Sonnets*, for instance. The best critiques of my work have been in Michele Birch-Conery's dissertation; in Carolyn Wright's *Prairie Schooner* review; and in Barbara Drake's *Dictionary of Literary Biography* entry.

My version of Woolf's philosophy of anonymity comes from a radio interview with an actor: "If you hang in there long enough," he said, "they'll build the theater around you." That's how I manage to keep working. Since my years in Amherst teaching for the University of Massachusetts, I've experienced more positive input than heretofore. Readers are less inclined to say, "I like your poems, but I don't understand them." I occasionally get fan letters from the great Out There. But, just to keep me honest, I had a recent sobering experience with a signer for the hearing impaired. She explained that this was her first poetry reading assignment; that she had conferred with the festival president, and they were still baffled by some of the poems. I talked until my throat was raw, and I hadn't gotten beyond three poems. She wanted more time, but I had to decline. I needed my voice for the next day's reading. When the time arrived, she looked convincing. I don't know what she said I said, but it did occur to me that I'd like to have my book reviews in this medium—so reassuring. You know that something is going on because of all those gestures, but you are spared the interpretation. From now on, that's the way I'd like to have it because the visionary figures already have too much to say, and criticism intensifies their chatter.

Virginia Woolf's Mirror

Commenting on the necessity women are to men, on men's restlessness under criticism, Woolf writes, "For if she begins to tell the truth, the figure in the looking-glass shrinks; his fitness for life is diminished."[14] Although it is clear from reading the essay based on two lectures that Woolf had a rollicking time writing the piece, she was not without misgivings as the date for its publication approached:

> . . . I will here sum up my impressions before publishing *A Room of One's Own*. It is a little ominous that Morgan won't review it. It makes me suspect that there is a shrill feminine tone in it which my intimate friends will dislike. I forecast, then, that I shall get no criticism, except of the evasive jocular kind, from Lytton, Roger and Morgan; that the press will be kind and talk of its charm and sprightliness; also I shall be attacked for a feminist and hinted at for a Sapphist; Sybil will ask me to luncheon; I shall get a good many letters from young women. I am afraid it will not be taken seriously. Mrs. Woolf is so accomplished a writer that all she says makes easy reading. . . this very feminine logic. . . a book to be put in the hands of girls. I doubt that I mind very much. The Moths; but I think it is to be waves, is trudging along; and I have that to

refer to, if I am damped by the other. It is a trifle, I shall say; so it is; but I wrote it with ardour and conviction.[15]

She does not consider it a major work, but as she observes in another place, ". . . there are offices to be discharged by talent for the relief of genius: meaning that one has the play side; the gift when it is mere gift; and the gift when it is serious, going to business. And one relieves the other."[16]

Well, then, in an era when every woman would like to have a wife, "a woman without whom. . . ," how about a man to serve as looking-glass? I like to imagine Snow White and the Seven Dwarfs in a version elaborated for just such a need. The dwarfs are male, of course, and fancy themselves Snow White's protectors, but really, all they want is a pretty woman who will cook and clean, a woman like water who will take the shape of any container they devise. Then she will give back each dwarf's image, as Woolf says, at twice its normal size. Every day the dwarfs work faithfully in the mines. *This poem of mine. . . This idea of mine. . . This critical opinion of mine. . .* until Snow White wants to escape to a room of her own. She has done her homework, she has salted away five hundred pounds. But her looking-glass duties demand more and more energy, what with seven men preening at all hours. She barely has time to dust their collection of traditional male authors and polish her cosmetic surface so that when the men look they will see what they want to see: themselves enlarged, filling every available opening.

When she tries for a turn at the mirror, all she sees is a dwarf. Some days she is tempted to add a little strychnine to their porridge, but that would, no doubt, come under the heading of unfair trade practices. Most judges are men: they would rule against her. Snow White begins to plot her escape from this *ménage à huit.* She is beginning to lose weight and is seriously depressed.

Doc diagnoses her problem. "Women have always been too emotional," he says, and he doesn't mean Eliot's *significant* emotion. "It's nothing a little sunshine won't cure." He prescribes aspirin, tells her she's been reading too much. "Why don't you take the kids to the zoo or bake some pies or go back to that fancy needlework you started months ago?"

That's exactly it, Snow White thinks. She feels as unimaginative as a mother-hen. She needs something besides this incessant clucking and crowing—a golden egg, perhaps; anything to wake up her mind and challenge her pen.

One morning when the dwarfs have left for work, and the dirty dishes groan and grumble from the kitchen sink, Snow White dawdles over a second cup of coffee while reading a book of Sappho's poems. She has smuggled the book into the house when the dwarfs weren't looking. That evening Snoopy discovers the book, face down on her nightstand, and wants to know what she's doing with "that trash." "If you insist on turning pages when you should be cooking, cleaning, or taking care of the children," he says, "why not take up Pindar or Anacreon?" He offers to find them for her on the shelf.

The New Mirror

Near the end of *A Writer's Diary* in 1840, only three months before her suicide, Virginia Woolf writes:

> I actually opened Matthew Arnold and copied. . . lines. While doing so, the idea came to me that why I dislike, and like, so many things idiosyncratically now, is because of my growing detachment from the hierarchy, the patriarchy.[17]

Even as I write, the tradition is being reshaped, and women are coming into their own—not as quickly as we might wish, but it is happening. The Mirror of Tradition will begin to reflect more women and image them more truly, partly because of the pioneering work of Virginia Woolf. Women found a small opening, wriggled through, learned craft and boldness from their male models, and struck out on their own to forge new forms for the content that had found so little place in literature. If the new subject matter had few male admirers at first, it found an overwhelming response from women readers. The younger women are already achieving distinction as poets and critics; the language is being revised to be more inclusive; more and more role models are becoming available for women and persons of color.

Years ago, Dorothy Donnelly published a long poem, "Trio in a Mirror," in *Poetry* magazine. The situation in the poem presents the reader with a chamber group of quite ordinary men performing near a large wall mirror. The theme has to do with the transformative power of art—on the creator (or interpreter) and on the audience, the co-creators. Donnelly incorporates most of the mirror lore of the Western tradition: a parade of gazers from Narcissus to Alice and a bevy of reflective surfaces from turtle shells ("a terrapin's carapace") to the Goose Girl's well. Although most of us have had enough of being goose girls, we wouldn't mind owning, or even producing, a few golden eggs. With persistence and luck and with the new vision made possible by more accurate mirrors, such recognition may at last come about through what Donnelly calls seeing new in "the burning-glass of [our] concentration."[18]

NOTES

1. *A Writer's Diary*, ed. Leonard Woolf (New York: Harcourt Brace Jovanovich, 1954), p. 196.

2. Northrop Frye, *T. S. Eliot* (New York: Grove Press, 1963), p. 29.

3. *Interviews with Contemporary Writers: Second Series, 1972-1982*, ed. L. S. Dembo (Madison: U. of Wisconsin Press, 1983), pp. 311-13.

4. "The Music of Poetry" (Third W. P. Ker Memorial Lecture at Glasgow University, 1942), in *Poets on Poetry*, ed. Charles Norman (New York: The Free Press, 1966), p. 334.

5. *Writer's Diary*, p. 220.

6. Ibid., pp. 220-21.

7. "Writing from Our Lives: A Vehicle for Change," *Canadian Woman Studies*, Vol. 12, No. 3 (Spring 1992), p. 106.

8. *A Room of One's Own*. (New York: Harcourt, Brace and World, 1957), p. 35.

9. Ibid., p. 36.

10. (New York: McGraw-Hill, 1972), p. xxxvi.

11. *Writer's Diary*, pp. 303-304.

12. Ibid., pp. 346-47.

13. Ibid., pp. 308-309.

14. *A Room of One's Own*, p. 36.

15. *Writer's Diary*, p. 145.

16. Ibid., p. 134.

17. Ibid., pp. 346-47.

18. Dorothy Donnelly, *Trio in a Mirror* (Tucson: U. of Arizona Press, 1960), p. 3.

THE TRADITION OF MARGINALITY

Kathleen Fraser

> *On the outside, you attempt to conform to an order which is alien to you. Exiled from yourself, you fuse with everything you encounter. You mime whatever comes near you. You become whatever you touch. In your hunger to find yourself, you move indefinitely far from yourself. . . . Assuming one model after another, one master after another, changing your face, form and language according to the power that dominates you. Sundered. . .*
> Luce Irigaray, "When Our Lips Speak Together"

> *As a representative of purity, moral, ideological, intellectual, or anything else, I am a walking lie. My own work and that of the women I admire gives its allegiance to the messiness of experience.*
> Nina Auerbach, "Engorging the Patriarchy"

> *Radium's radioactivity was so great that it could not be ignored. It seemed to contradict the principle of conservation of energy and thereby forced a reconsideration of the foundation of physics.*
> Encyclopedia Britannica

When I was in second grade, my Aunt Dottie came to visit. She was a tall, glamorous brunette who worked as an executive secretary for Western Union. Also she smoked cigarettes and had no husband or children. These things immediately defined her in my mind as a separate category of female from my mother who, as wife of a Presbyterian minister and mother of four closely spaced children, represented a world of benevolent oppression. While Aunt Dottie rested and bathed before dinner, we children had to be quiet because this was her vacation. Each night she appeared at our modest dining table in her long red velvet dressing gown, trailing perfume and powder. For me, the single most powerful event of her two-week stay was the evening she took my mother and me off to the movies to see *Madame Curie*, starring Greer Garson, at the Orpheum Theatre in downtown Tulsa. We arrived in the late, dim afternoon but when we emerged the world was dark and sharp with perspective. We were taken to a fancy restaurant for club sandwiches and chocolate sodas, and what followed was probably my first conversation with women about possibility and probability.

Madame Curie has been described by a contemporary of hers as "a pale, timid little woman in black cotton dress, with the saddest face I had ever looked upon." But Greer Garson's face—a study in curiosity, humor, intelligence, and determination—will always take Curie's visual place in my mind. It was to Garson's face and Curie's quest that I turned, increasingly hooked as she lived out her life on screen, searching for that element which had not yet been imagined or named.

In the movie, Madame Curie has obstacle after obstacle to surmount, including the overwhelming disdain of the all-male French scientific community. Her arduous tasks are on the scale of Psyche's, as she sorts through a ton of pitchblende to come up with one-tenth of a gram of uncontaminated radium chloride. The tension builds through endless failures in the lab, as she uses what has been proposed by traditional scientific method thus far, then finally discards it to consult the further reaches of her imagination for what might work. Halfway through the film, her husband Pierre, who has worked side by side with her, is killed in a street accident and she is left alone and grief-stricken. Still, she persists in her obsession, spending long hours in the lab, even though the pads of her thumbs are growing numb from the powerful effects of the radioactive substance.

Everything now seems to be in black and white. She spends endless days and nights sitting before the microscope, trying this solution and that, with no sign of significant results. Then one night, in exhaustion, she returns to the lab to check her experiments, and, before she can turn on the light, she sees a faint glow coming from one of the saucers where her chemical solutions are waiting. It is radium, giving off that light. It is the glowing evidence that she has been seeking. It is like nothing that has come before it. It has eluded her for years. Curie finds, ultimately, that, unlike phosphorescence, radium is not dependent upon an outside source of energy but appears to arise spontaneously from the uranium itself—an unheard-of departure from the known laws of nature.

I remembered this image when talking with a friend about our first female role models. I realized that mine was Madame Curie, looking for the imagined light in the dark of her lab. There weren't a lot of women role models after that, certainly not among the poets I was taught. The few samples of ladylike grace offered up in junior high were not for me. I wrote a bit of doggerel and a bit more of private seriousness, but essentially had been well trained to fear poetry. I resented its refusal to give over any meanings other than those few handed down by my teachers. Although my career plan was to be a journalist, I attended Occidental, a reputable liberal arts college where we read the great literature and philosophy and heard lectures on "The History of Civilization" every morning for two years running, delivered in the college chapel, where we all were seated on long church pews taking notes or writing comments back and forth to each other.

In these two years, there were no women-authored texts on the reading list. This absence had its effect and made its point subliminally clear. Several of my women friends began writing poetry and would pass their new poems around during the more boring lectures. Thus poetry actively reentered my life through my peers—a kind of resistance movement going on in the third row; suddenly it seemed intriguing. Within a year, I found myself secretly scribbling. I would type my final versions sitting on the floor of the girls' shower room late at night so as not to disturb my roommate, then rush to Civ lecture to send my first efforts down the chapel pew and back.

For my birthday, senior year, my friends gave me T. S. Eliot's *Collected Poems*, William Carlos Williams' *Journey to Love*, e. e. cummings' *Six Non-lectures*, and García Lorca's *Selected Poems*. I felt deeply shy and thrilled. My barely emerging identity was being acknowledged with this act of recognition. I switched majors from philosophy to English literature. Very little of that major included modern poetry; certainly, there were no women poets discussed. When I graduated, I did not know of the work of Marianne Moore or H. D. or Gertrude Stein. I somehow got hold of

Virginia Woolf on my own and was pulled further into poetry by reading *The Waves*.

My first poems tried to model themselves on what I was reading—the dark presentiments of Eliot, the surreal lyrics of Lorca, and a few sudden untranslatable intensities inspired by Dylan Thomas. I tried to effect an e. e. cummings homage with-out its looking too derivative. I was deeply attracted by his refusal to conform to the conventional syntax and grammar of acceptable mainstream poetry. Cummings' passionate resistance would align itself in my mind with Madame Curie's refusal to give up her belief in the possibility of a new element. Already, I was aware that I carried a number of clamoring voices in me, arguing, protesting, obsessively repeating themselves. . . my mind was polyphonic and fragmenting, as I heard it, split between my resolve to be an attractive and acceptable female student, and my stubborn resistance to all rules—including those of prosody, which did not appear to describe my hesitant and multiple ways of perceiving and forming thought. All was shifting ground and formally suspect.

Soon after graduation, I left to pursue my career in journalism, in New York City, where I quickly met several budding poets who suggested I join a writing workshop. One woman, a black poet who signed her manuscripts G. Oden to prevent sexist prejudgments of her work, invited me to a reading given by Stanley Kunitz. I was thrilled by his Yeatsian language and passionate metaphysical vision and signed up for his poetry workshop at the YMHA Poetry Center, learning through him to admire the genderless and splendid work of Elizabeth Bishop. I also acquired the skills to write a certain kind of good poem, of which I sold three to *The New Yorker*, several years later. During this workshop period, we began hearing of Sylvia Plath through Kunitz and Robert Lowell. In 1962, we read her poems; by 1963, she was dead. Plath was my first female role model in poetry. The male poets and editors were in love with her. Lowell read her poems at his reading. Not only did she have the superb craft and ear, but there was clearly something seductive for the male literary world in her "madness" and her tragic end.

It turned out that there *were* a few other women writing poetry. In the early sixties I happened upon several wonderfully intelligent poems by Adrienne Rich in *The Nation*. In 1963, I heard of a two-week summer workshop being taught by a woman poet unknown to me—Daisy Alden. I decided to spend my vacation studying with her, though I'd never read a word of her work. Something in me yearned for a female role model, for a teacher who could show how one might attempt to be in the world, as a woman poet, without choosing nervous breakdown, total isolation, or suicide as a solution.

When I arrived at the workshop, we were told that Daisy Alden was sick and that our teacher would be Kenneth Koch. Koch was on the attack; he cut down any sign of high seriousness or emotional vulnerability, in the person or the poem. I did recover from him the playful attitude towards poetic language that I'd loved in my father's recitations of Lewis Carroll and various nonsense verse; also, we were taught a certain skepticism towards sentimental poetic retreads. That was healthy. Through Koch, I met Frank O'Hara, and through O'Hara, Barbara Guest, whose poetry and person he admired enormously.

While O'Hara's energetic celebration of the whole of life in its dailiness was a great permission-giver, it was Guest's linguistic mysteries that lingered, composed and collaged from the precise fragments of her painterly witness and her skeptical wariness of language's confinement and oversimplification. Barbara Guest was the only woman poet in the first generation of the New York School. When the second generation emerged, full of ego and ambition, a major anthology of the works of the New York School came out, in 1970, edited by David Shapiro, around twenty-three at the time, and Ron Padgett, in his late twenties. Barbara Guest, who had been a major figure in the painting and poetry scene through the fifties and sixties, who had been publishing her poems and art criticism in many New York School magazines and reading on various New York School programs, and who had published at least four books of poems by then, was left out of the anthology. A friend of Shapiro and Padgett explained to me later: "We didn't think her work was that interesting." Meanwhile, twenty-six men were included in that anthology, some of them brilliant poets, such as Edwin Denby and James Schuyler, but others merely adequate camp followers. One very young woman from the third generation—Bernadette Mayer, an original experimentalist—was included. Guest's erasure was my first in-person encounter with this common historic practice.

Through the sixties, various movements emerged and ran parallel courses, all sharing two observable similarities. They each had male theorists setting forth the new aesthetic dogma—usually asserted in published letters or theoretical repudiations of other existing poetics—and each of them had its own woman poet. Few women writers seemed interested in helping to change that ratio. It was not difficult to see that there was only so much room for women at the top. Under the fatherly aegis of W. C. Williams and Robert Duncan, Denise Levertov's poems received serious critical attention. Anne Sexton followed sadly after Plath, baffling East Coast critics who were both intrigued and appalled by her confessions of emotional instability. In the group around Jack Spicer, Joanne Kyger was acknowledged, if minimally. Diane DiPrima, as sister figure of the Beats, was known for publishing many knowns and unknowns in her mimeo magazine, *Floating Bear*. Gwendolyn Brooks was the token black woman, but her work was not widely known or taught in the white community; Carolyn Kizer, under Kunitz's mentorship, was admired for her finely pitched, celebratory lyrics and translations from the Chinese, but her major poetic satire, "Pro Femina," was not sufficiently appreciated until a later generation. The idea that few women really write poetry was still popularly accepted.

This list is, of course, an oversimplification and leaves out many names, but it is a kind of topological map of certain formations that were rising clearly enough to be noticed. There were others, innocently conspiring in their own *non*recognition. We literary women have all been taught our manners and, with few exceptions in the sixties, women sent out their work and waited to be taken up by powerful male editors and mentors who were willing to discover them and authenticate their reality as writers. Women mentors were in short supply, still captured by their own tentative power base.

One might speculate that such neglect gave women poets a kind of freedom from the confines of public approval and aesthetic directive to develop their own unique voices. And that may be true, in part. On the other hand, like most serious artists, we wanted to materialize, to be heard and acknowledged as authentic by some outside recognition. We needed a readership.

What were young women poets to do, understanding clearly by then the rules of the game and how we must submit our language to the scrutiny of those in power? What if we carried in us the seeds of a rebellion that didn't want to follow the leader; what if we wanted to write, unhampered by group worship of whatever aesthetic theory was in current vogue; to cross boundaries and give voice to impurities involving shifting grounds of feeling and intellect? We *were* learning and selecting what we could from each encountered poet and teacher. But there was something more, glowing in the dark. We didn't know what to name it yet, but some of us wanted to locate a poetics on our own terms. We had always been the marginalized sex, looking towards the center, and from our point of view there was reporting yet to be done.

For me, the awakening began out of some combination of Simone de Beauvoir's call to consciousness in *The Second Sex*, Adrienne Rich's grave and alarming poem "The Roofwalker," and Barbara Guest's tenacious insistence on the primacy of reinventing language structures in order to catch one's own at-oddness with the presumed superiority of the central mainstream vision. Quietly, at first, then very actively, variations of this perception began to surface. The women's movement came on strong, and poetry was at the center of it. Finally, one imagined, there would be a warm room where the multiple styles of women's minds and bodies and poetic languages could flower. But, in fact, something else happened. There were political needs—raw, bottled-up feelings wanting out—and a call for the immediately accessible language of personal experience as a binding voice of women's strength. Many women focused on the poem as a place for self-expression, for giving a true account, for venting rage, and for embracing sexual love of women. The lesbian political vision became particularly potent and powerful in writing; the suddenly perceived freedom of women to claim their power through their love and support of one another could no longer be denied. So powerful were their voices that a new center evolved in the seventies, a poetics organized and dominated by the aesthetic vision of women-centered literary magazines, such as *Sinister Wisdom, 13th*

Moon, and *Conditions*—often lesbian and separatist in ideology and almost exclusively focused on poems of content that described and reinforced the values and life-styles shared by this community.

It was in the early stages of this forming center that I came to San Francisco, an emerging yet vocally timid feminist, to direct the Poetry Center and to teach at San Francisco State. These were probably the loneliest years of my writing life. I knew many poets, but, although I enjoyed some as social friends, I had no true community. I no longer wanted to "submit" work to abstract male editors and try calmly to absorb their well-meaning but patronizing "corrections" of my work. And yet it seemed clear to me that my work would not be deemed appropriate for lesbian-feminist magazines.

In that necessary but painful phase of feminism in the seventies, heterosexual women were often regarded as politically untrustworthy, despite their intense friendships with women and their activism on behalf of the women's community. Also, there was the problem of one's interest in nontraditional poetic voices. I'd long since been compelled by the linguistic inventions of Gertrude Stein and by Virginia Woolf's complex interior monologues—the resistance and playfulness of dictions peculiarly odd, peculiarly *at odds* with standard "accessible" modes of expression in poems and prose works.

I recognized a structural order of fragmentation and resistance to the patriarchal models that confirmed my perspective. I wanted this difference in my own work. Yet, ironically, this fascination with the innovative works of modernist women writers marginalized me even further from the official women's writing community. I continued to write, but I very seldom sent work to magazines.

Eventually, during my stint as director of the Poetry Center at San Francisco State, I got to know several women poets whose work and thought became increasingly important to me. Their focus brought me to a different kind of attentiveness: it wasn't the witty polish or posturing of "great lines," but a listening attitude, an attending to unconscious connections, a backing-off of the performing ego to allow the mysteries of language to come forward and resonate more fully. It was at this time that I began seriously reading H. D., Jack Spicer, and George Oppen. Theirs was quite a different attitude towards poetry than I'd absorbed in New York. I was stimulated to reach further into the silence of my own work.

I began to meet rather regularly with two women poets—Frances Jaffer and Beverly Dahlen—to read and criticize our own poetry and to discuss our growing involvement with feminist practice and how it converged with our writing. We shared our uncomfortable feelings of marginality vis-à-vis the women's writing community and our attraction to the various writings coming out of the modernist project. Our collective female experience of multiplicity and fragmentation and our wanting to locate that, structurally, in the look and sound of our poems seemed to find a sympathetic tradition there, as well as support for our resistance to certain academic emphases with which we were not in tune.

We began to talk increasingly about whether there might be a difference between female and male perception, located in the language men and women choose to express their perceptions. Not that the three of us wrote alike, but it did appear that there was growing evidence of certain gender-oriented preoccupations and distinctions. Our shared aesthetic and political concerns began making increasingly rigorous demands upon us, causing us all to become more intellectually exacting and artistically inventive in our writings. I do believe that without each other's support at that time, none of us would have written as much or as well. But the more we wrote, the less we fit in—to anything. In our shared ideology and our poetic practice, we were not pure: neither purely, categorically avant-garde nor purely one kind of feminist, Marxist, Freudian, or Lacanian. All these directions had their pull in us and stimulated work.

But the questions remained—where could we send our work? Sometimes a few wishful fantasies of making our own magazine surfaced, but no one could quite imagine adding that labor to already demanding work schedules. A year or so went by without our meeting as a group. We each had things to sort out in our own lives and writing. I also think that in a certain sense we were treading water when it came to our continually voiced unhappiness at feeling the lack of a definable audience. We parted as a writing group, without parting as friends, in an unresolved drift towards privacy that felt both necessary and frustrating. I went to

Europe for six months, and getting away gave me distance and time to think. All our conversations echoed in my mind. Our isolation as writers was a dilemma I could neither let go of nor find a solution for.

When I got back in the fall of 1982, I was scheduled to teach a course called "Feminist Poetics," which I'd introduced into the Creative Writing Department curriculum in order to consider, within the community of a classroom, the very questions that had been pressing upon me for years. Why was there no acknowledged tradition of modernist women's poetry continuing out of H. D., Stein, Dorothy Richardson, Woolf, Mina Loy, Djuna Barnes, Laura Riding, Lorine Niedecker, and Marianne Moore, as there clearly was for men working out of the Pound-Williams tradition or the Stevens-Auden lineage? Why had most of the great women modernists been dropped cold from reading lists and university curricula?

Why were most feminist and traditional critics failing to develop any interest in contemporary women poets working to bring structural and syntactic innovation into current poetic practice?

Then there were the puzzling questions of language and gender, which were being argued convincingly, often from opposite positions. Did female experience require a totally different language, as Luce Irigaray seemed to be suggesting? How was that difference located in usage, a usage that had perhaps occurred and been ignored, dismissed as insignificant, or dropped out of the canon and quickly absorbed—even appropriated—by powerful figures such as Pound and Graves? How is gender expressed and imprinted socially? Teaching this class raised my distress level as it simultaneously gave me strength of purpose. Something more had to be done. There was a conversation with the writer Bob Gluck that sticks in my mind. It began with the above symptoms of distress and finished, for me, with his gentle but clear statement: "Kathleen, you must decide who your audience is and then address it." He was not talking about the private act of writing.

I went away again for the summer with that sentence dogging me, and my resolve became clear. I began formulating a tentative plan for a modest-size journal, which I hoped to lure Frances and Bev into being part of. I missed our particular way of talking and the feeling of support that came from it. There was no longer any question in my mind; I had to give time to making a place where our issues could be aired and some new choices put forward in women's poetry—asserted and selected by women—including a revival of modernist figures and a closer look at contemporary work discounted by critics. I wanted a serious yet not a formal conversation among poets and critics. I wrote to my critic friend, Annette Kolodny, and asked her if such a project seemed of use to her. I wanted to know if she thought it would be taken seriously by the feminist critics, whom we poets were reading but whom we imagined as a fairly insular group with little interest in what were, for us, burning issues. I suggested to her that maybe women critics simply didn't know how to begin thinking or talking about the more innovative compositional work and the seriousness of its quest. Perhaps there was some fear. I wondered if it would be of help if the poets themselves were asked to write "working notes" about their work process and to do informal commentary on books by other women; perhaps new insights and descriptions coming directly from the poets might provide useful clues for the careful detective work in which scholar-critics engage. Annette answered immediately, agreeing with all these speculations and assuring me that she would welcome such an attempt. Her letter was the final encouragement I needed. I returned to San Francisco and talked with Frances; she was ready. We called Bev, who also agreed. I suggested that we try to enlist, as contributing editors, two feminist critics whose essays we'd been reading and discussing in our writing group and who had become friends in the process— Carolyn Burke and Rachel Blau DuPlessis. Two years into our venture Beverly withdrew, and a young poet-scholar, Susan Gevirtz, brought new editorial energy to our enterprise.

That's the gestation part. But to show what a collective labor it was to name our journal, let me share my notes on our first meeting, in which we were searching for a name that would identify us clearly as a journal with a different perspective. The ideas came flying fast, as in a jazz improvisation of three instruments, where one voice comments on the phrase played by another, a movement of call and response, until some new resolution of the classic tune has been achieved. The suggestions started with *Parts of Speech*, then *Feminine Endings* (after Judy Grahn's poem), then *Indefinite Article*, then *Text/ure*, then *Alice Blue Gown*, then *Red Tulips*, then

Para/phrase, then *Where (we) are,* then *I (too)*—as in Marianne Moore's line about poetry: "I, too, dislike it"—and finally *HOW(ever),* from her next line, "However, there is a place for it." First, *However* was one word; then we broke it into its typographical and parenthetical components. The name represented for us an addendum, a point of view from the margins, meant to flesh out what had thus far been proposed in poetry and poetics.

There were problems in asserting a point of view that defined itself as female and often feminist, and in making a magazine devoted solely to the publication of women writers. Some people inevitably felt excluded, as seems to happen whenever a new aesthetic is asserted publicly. Given the territorial bias we've all been subjected to in Western culture, the expectation of exclusion seems almost automatically programmed in. But rather than seeing ourselves as exclusionary or here to displace or replace anything or anyone, we hoped, instead, to be an added source of information and stimulation. One thinks of Dada, Surrealism, Futurism, Black Mountain, the New York School, and recent Language-centered propositions, and one knows that there is plenty of room for exploration of multiplicity in poetry and theory being practiced by women, without destroying our basic support of one another. The reward for asserting a vision is to become visible, to participate actively in the wider literary conversation and to help in creating a community that has been waiting to come into view. It turns out, in our case, that there have been many women like us feeling isolated for years, excluded from the aesthetic or political mandates of existing poetics.

There is another question, raised by Johanna Drucker in a talk at the Cannessa Park Gallery in San Francisco, and, in a different way, by Nina Auerbach in her paper, "Engorging the Patriarchy," delivered at the Cal Tech conference on "Marxism and Feminism." Both Auerbach and Drucker address the potentially dangerous position into which women writers may put themselves by continuing to see themselves as marginal—either in their use of language or in specific, characteristic styles of living, writing, or thinking. Both fear that in attempting to explore or even define a new terrain, we may be cutting ourselves off from access to the patriarchy (or, in our case, the matriarchy as well)—the existing power lines and energy sources clearly necessary to our survival. Drucker suggests that we ought no longer to identify our differences, but should merge with "the genderless project of literature" and take our places confidently, rather than spend more time writing a scenario of difference and marginality.

Auerbach sees that "feminist ideology is inseparable from the lived knowledge of subordination, just as reading and writing are part of our continual self-authorizations and self-authentication."[1] She wants us to enter into the discourse, so as to deflate the phantasmic powers we have projected onto our subordinators and begin to see them more in scale as flawed individuals asserting their ideas. But she warns that any form of discourse perceived, even if not intended, as separatist is always a double-edged sword: the very qualities that women are praised for having, *then* risk becoming an institutionalized enterprise, rigidly enforced, and prohibiting the edge of difference from continuing to find its ever-changing voice. She is afraid that if we make too absolute a definition of uniformity and uniqueness of women's writing, we will be quickly embraced and as quickly absorbed and effaced by well-meaning critics, only to disappear with Zelda Fitzgerald and Dorothy Wordsworth into the footnotes of self-proclaimed male truths. As she suggests:

> Our stress on our uniformity and uniqueness in culture may make us look frailer and more boring than we are.... Our own complicity in this isolation may invite scholars to define us in reductive formulas they do not apply to more intimately known material.... [It] may make us. . . appear too special for the gross machinery of scholarship.[2]

While I take seriously these voiced fears, they arrive at a time when I am experiencing a new inner strength and integration from activity I see not as separatist but, more accurately, as shedding light upon a burgeoning group of women poets—poets who are unique though quite definitely *not* uniform, and who have consistently been neglected by academic, mainstream, feminist, *and* avant-garde critics. Instead of waiting to be approved by this or that established authority (or invited into the dance by an imagined mentor), we've engaged in urgent sifting and digging, meaning to reconstruct that pre-existing tradition of modernist women who need us to acknowledge them as much as we need them to fall back on for daring and spiritual renewal, so that *we* may set out a light for whatever next unknown voices are laboring in the dark.

It is from this assertion of a point of view, through the editing of *HOW(ever)*, that I began to demystify for myself the forms of power, the totems and secret caves of taste-making in the literary world. It is precisely in proposing a poetics of sufficient depth and complexity to satisfy our own hungers—as well as participating in the "dig" for a female tradition of language inventiveness—that we begin to starve the larger-than-life figures who have dominated and denied us. Not only do we exorcise their neglect, but we understand the commitment and hard work they have brought to the literatures they've found valuable. Thus, from that edge or brink or borderline we call the margin, we are able to create another center. . . a laboratory in which to look for the unknown elements we suspect are there.

NOTES

This paper was delivered as a talk at The Poetry Project, St. Mark's in the Bowery, New York City, June 1985. It also appeared in *Frontiers: A Special Issue, Women and Words*, Vol. X, No. 3 (Boulder: U. of Colorado, 1989).

1. Nina Auerbach, "Engorging the Patriarchy," in *Feminist Issues in Literary Scholarship,* ed. Shari Benstock (Bloomington: Indiana U. Press, 1987), p. 152.

2. Ibid., p. 157.

The *New* New Poetry Handbook

Debora Greger

> If a man understands a poem,
> he shall have troubles.
> —Mark Strand

If a woman understands a poem,
nothing is changed.
                    —Virginia Samuelson

WRITING WITH THE SUN

Joy Harjo

Everything merged those early summer mornings I escaped our heavy house before anyone else awakened in that most silent place before dawn. There was a stillness at that hour throughout the land, as the damp earth shivered in anticipation of the sun. The sun made ready to climb the eastern horizon. In this time of peace, of refuge, I would dig to smell and touch the dark earth near the foundation of the house, that which was mother to my spirit. I would make things of the earth, and sing—my own gift to the struggle as was the chirrupping of the birds, the rhythmic clip of insects, the arabesque of the dragonfly—who all wished to be named *morning*. We helped call the sun up. And in turn the sun called to us.

That combination of voices was poetry, and therein was my first understanding of poetry. All living things were linked by this transformation, from the cadence of a wind through the flowering bushes to the natural dips and curves of the earth traveling out in all directions from the center of the world. This was my unspeakable happiness. Spirit interacted with grace. I was no longer trapped in the clumsy physical, or in the way of the television. There was an unbroken connection between the process of the creation of the world and a child's human spirit.

There are words I remember hearing precisely for the first time. "Accident" I heard as I stood in the backseat of my father's car as we traveled to a destination other than the grocery store. It was always quite an event to ride somewhere unknown. If it was summer we usually went to the lake, otherwise to visit relatives or friends. I was usually the first one to answer the sound of the motor, the first one in the car. I loved to travel the earth, the earth that fed me with songs.

That afternoon I had either spilled something or was on the verge of an accident of spilling. The word "accident" emerged from the current of talking as a shiny, intriguing object of sound and space. The new word grew from my tongue as if I had invented it, and perhaps I had reinvented it by turning it over in my mouth. I took it in as the sun took all of us in when we participated in the ceremony of sunrise. I spoke the word like a secret, over and over again until the word lost any meaning, and folded back into the place in which we are all related: walking and flying insects, trees and bushes, beloved earth, humans and the sun.

I don't remember the first time I heard the word "poetry." I flip back through smells of chalk and wax, through disinfectant and ink. The word "poetry" is a shadowy figure, walking into view, a familiar stranger waiting for me to come around the corner. Perhaps the word was always there, relaxing in the cortex of memory, waving from the foreground of my particular pattern of DNA. Other words and concepts quickly passed through my life. I collected and stored them for reference, but poetry lingered as something I had in mind, a something that smelled like the ocean, or dark earth sifted through my hands so early in the morning.

On my eighth birthday I was given a Louis Untermyer collection of poetry for children. I was surprised my mother had read my secret desire for books of poetry. We had no books in our home except for a Bible my mother gave me when I began attending church for the singing and storytelling. Later, I brought home books from the library. My mother had an eighth grade education from a one-room school in northwestern Arkansas. Eighth grade was all that could be afforded in clothes and shoes for her or for the six boys in the family. The children were needed for labor; books were a luxury. The only book she had in her home was a family Bible which was used as a repository of information on births and deaths, not for poetry or stories.

My mother quoted a William Blake poem once from memory, a poem she'd been forced to memorize at school. From her recitation I understood that the poem was foreign to her, from a place and time that excluded her. But then her memories of school were painful. She was teased for her ragged clothes, her lard pail lunches of biscuits, lard and water gravy. Education meant fist fights and embarrassment. Yet, I understood that she loved poetry. This was poetry, this stuff of sound and grace. But it was her singing to the radio that made me understand her love of poetry. I listened more closely then to the rattling whistle of the world. I made my own songs in the dark. When she gave me the gift of a book of poetry she must have recognized that particular hunger burning me, for it lit her heart as she wrote songs long after the children were asleep.

It's at this age I associate poetry with books, with words printed precisely on the page in perfect rows. I've forgotten talking to the sun. I am a prodigious reader and prolific artist, yet the words appear to belong to someone else. I stumble over them, duck, and avoid confrontation. My identity is eaten up by fear. I don't know where to place myself in these classes of students who are predominantly white. There are a few Indian students here and there. We are the largest minority, but we don't wish to call attention to ourselves. I don't know how to speak. It becomes a problem. Notes are sent home to my parents. Maybe I don't give them the notes, or they don't have time to respond, or my mother is too intimidated to deal with school officials. My parents divorce and my mother works two and sometimes three jobs. I eventually handle all school correspondence for my brothers and sister and myself. Poetry belongs to someone else. It's a tradition that belongs to the other children.

One poem stands out from the struggle of those times. Emily Dickinson spoke to me from winged pages: "I'm nobody, who are you?/Are you nobody, too?" Her voice penetrated the soft wet earth of the bog beneath the wordlessness, loosened the fertile underground in the place of great losses. Poetry was revealed as a sacred language, something I didn't find in the church and Sunday school I attended alone and then with my sister. It was a gift from a woman who searched out her own truth in the judgmental Puritan enclave of this country. The images called sacred were constructed for her by the fathers and the church. She was no place to be found in those unrelenting places, but there in her room where the sun came in to speak those rare mornings she met herself and the poetry that became her.

Yet the distilled and potent image of poetry from the sum total of my education—from the Tulsa public schools, church, and Indian boarding school—an image that followed me into the university when I decided to become first a surgeon, a painter, and then a poet was this: a man in a tweed coat with a grey beard on a face pale from little sun recites obscure verses in an institute of stern brick. He is unapproachable. His poems have nothing to do with the intricate images of my life as a Muscogee woman from Oklahoma, of a people who were exiled from their homelands by people who spoke his language.

When I came to poetry it was through the struggles of tribal peoples to assert our human rights, to secure our sovereign rights as nations in the early seventies. It was the struggle begun by my grandmothers and grandfathers when they fought the move from our homelands in the Southeast to Indian Territory. This, too, was my personal struggle as a poet. It was in this wave of cultural renaissance for Indian peoples in this country that I heard the poetry that would change me, a poetry that could have been written those mornings of creation from childhood. This poetry named me as it jolted the country into sharp consciousness.

I heard the poetry of Simon Ortiz, an Acoma Pueblo poet who wrote of the sacred in the everyday; the poetry of Leslie Silko from Laguna Pueblo, whose stunning images still run through my bloodstream; of Scott Momaday, from the Kiowa people, who was in love with words and the land that made them. Their poetry is of this land, a land that mothers all those who step out onto the earth from between their mothers' legs. The land had fed each of us, clothed us, blessed us.

I found my poetic sensibility through the work of African poets, in particular Okot B' Pitek's *Song of Lawino*. It speaks of similar struggles of a colonized people through the song of Lawino, a tribal woman from Uganda who is the angry consciousness of mothers who tally the destruction in their bodies; she is the earth speaking.

The parallel struggle of women to identify and claim power in a world that disrespected my mother and all women, outside as well as within the Christianized elements of my tribe, and to write with a language particular to our experience also formed me. I honed my words against this sword of contention and worked to create my own language out of language of exclusion. Emily Dickinson and Phillis Wheatley led this struggle, as well as the *Beloved Woman* of the Cherokee people, Nancy Ward, whose words made policy, changed everything. The poetry and lives of Adrienne Rich and Audre Lorde continue to reshape the destiny of women in this century, as does the work of Leslie Silko.

When I went to that which named me, made me sing, a shift occurred with the same force as a continental shift that creates volcanoes, sets off earthquakes. The effect wasn't particularly noticeable at first; there were a few strains, some breaks and losses. The coming changes swirled and baked in the underground while a generation went through college, worked, took care of children, cleaned house, and continued to define us as Indian (specifically tribal), woman, man, and human. Our poetry embraces this revolution.

I used to be intimidated by the image of the poet who glanced sternly at me now and then from the worn pages of his book of poetry, a book that excluded Leslie, Okot, or anyone like me. I have encountered him in the institutions in which I've taught, lectured, and performed. He is harsh and changeless in a world that constantly changes. He and his poetry have a place here, but that place is *with* us, not above us. This world is a song, a large poem we are all working on together, Alice Walker has said. We are all linked together in this song that rejuvenates culture, that changes us as we climb to the sun.

THE AUTOMATIC WOMAN

Gwen Head

Author. War.

One word is as bright and mysterious as *angel*, the other anxious and dreadful as *worry*. Both are heard often in the French Quarter apartment at 830 Bourbon Street where I live with my parents. I like words, enjoy collecting and displaying them. And *author* is the word of all words. It is what my father (who is a *newspaperman, slot man* on the *copy desk* of *The Times-Picayune*) most admires, so it is what I want to be when I grow up. But *war* is a problem. It compels my silence every evening at eight when Gabriel Heatter comes on with radio news. It demands the saving of red and blue points for sugar and butter. It blackens the front page of the newspaper with big type and photos of mud, tanks, smashed-up airplanes. And of men, weary men in muddy uniforms, carrying rifles and hand grenades.

My father is too old to fight, but there are destroyers and minesweepers tied up along the Mississippi River docks where we walk on Sunday afternoons. And one weekend, a cousin by marriage comes to visit. He is a *major* wearing *combat ribbons*, pieces of brightly striped silk rep on a rigid backing. I want to play with the ribbons; I can't have them. Later my mother, holding me on her lap, opens the unabridged, India paper dictionary that is the biggest and most respected book in our household. Today we pass up Gems and Orchids, two of my favorites, and open at once to the color plate of Medals and Orders of Honor and Merit. She reads me their names: the Distinguished Flying Cross, from Great Britain ("that's another name for England"), the Iron Cross of Prussia ("that's what Germany used to be called"), and, most important because they are given by the United States of America to our own fighting boys, the Purple Heart and the Medal of Honor. The latter comes in two versions, one for the Army, one for the Navy. I wouldn't mind having these for dress-up, either. But you have to be very brave to win them—so brave you get *wounded* ("hurt very badly," says my mother) in combat to earn a Purple Heart, so brave that you're dead, or very near it, to win a Medal of Honor, which also seems to require saving the lives—the more the better—of other soldiers.

I am a cosseted only child, *petite, chataine,* and four years old in polyglot New Orleans. I know that women can be WACs and WAVEs. But it's hard to imagine women fighting in those snappy short-skirted uniforms, those sensible but high-heeled shoes. They don't fight, my mother assures me, sensing my fear. But the fear isn't about fighting; it's about *not* fighting. The syllogism forming in my pre-logical brain goes something like this: Authors write about important things. War is the most important thing in the world right now. As a girl, I will never be allowed to fight in a war.

And therefore I can never be an author.

This incident, a sudden and true *re-vision,* came back to me some months ago as I began trying to think seriously about myself and my place as a woman writer in a literary tradition made mostly by men and based almost entirely on their concerns. I thought I would go on to write about women who had mattered to me in early childhood: a strong woman principal, a ballet teacher, a concert pianist willing to take on bratty beginning students, and about how autonomous women vanished from my life when my family moved from the lively, bohemian French Quarter of New Orleans to the stultifying Southern gentility of San Antonio, Texas. There would follow my adolescent love of the piano, fostered by a gay man and by the active presence, on the international concert scene, of dazzling performers as diverse as Wanda Landowska and Rosalyn Tureck, Clara Haskil and Guiomar Novaes.

Then would come my discovery of the poetry of Yeats, soon to be followed by Baudelaire, Eliot, Stevens; my years of reading, travel, and attempts at writing; my first marriage and the birth of my daughter; and finally the crucial importance of the women's movement of the late sixties and early seventies both to the emergence of my work and to the eventual end of my first marriage.

And certainly there was—there is—a long list of books by women writers that *made things happen* for me and countless others: de Beauvoir's *The Second Sex*, Germaine Greer's *The Female Eunuch*, Gilbert and Gubar's *The Madwoman in the Attic*, Phyllis Chesler's *Women and Madness*, Kingston's *The Woman Warrior*; the poetry of Levertov, Rich, Plath, Sexton, and of Ai, Diane Wakoski, Eleanor Lerman. This outpouring of work by and about women had a visceral excitement that seems to me scarce in more recent work by women. Its technical brilliance was inseparable from its content; stunning literary skills helped women scold, shout, and sing, as well as build temples of reasoned argument that held firm above the fray. Books like these rattled the plate tectonics of personality; they picked up whole lives and set them down in new and surprising places.

In the midst of all this turbulence, the Supreme Court's ruling on *Roe v. Wade* made abortion legal; henceforward the reproductive freedom on which all other female freedoms depend seemed permanently assured. And the Equal Rights Amendment, a major goal for the National Organization for Women and other feminist organizations, appeared to be unstoppably headed toward ratification.

Thus when I returned to my old friendships with Sappho, Colette, Madame de Sevigné, it was suddenly clear that the history of Western women writing was a history of subversion, sedition, even outright revolution, wave after wave of it rolling through the centuries; and that this revolution had as its end not just the freeing of women from their traditional strictures and shackles, but the radical alteration, even the overthrow, of many hallowed ideas and institutions. Some of these battles then appeared to be won, or at least to be winnable; a new era of cooperation between the sexes seemed to be dawning.

Yes, it was exhilarating to look back. But in the present it seemed equally important to acknowledge the kind, concerned, sometimes overtly feminist men who are the husbands, colleagues, sons, and cherished friends of the mostly complaisant (and not a little complacent) women writing now. As for these women writers' futures, they had to be limitlessly rosy. For weren't they—we—now fully "liberated?"

But I found it inexplicably difficult to finish this essay along those lines. As deadlines came and went, it lay inert on the page. It wouldn't smile or scream, wouldn't kick or clap its hands. In a word, it was stillborn. While I was waiting for some miraculous midwife to come along and breathe life into it, my husband and I went to Paris. It was my first visit in twenty-eight years. We stayed in Neuilly, in the serene and spacious home of a pair of American psychiatrists who were living, meanwhile, in our house in Berkeley. That house swap, the serendipitous result of a three by five card on the bulletin board of our neighborhood grocery, turned out to be the midwife I was seeking. For situated in Neuilly is the Museum of Women and Automata. Here is a first reaction from my Paris journal, written at the end of a stifling day in July:

> Mid-afternoon we seize a breath of initiative and decide to go see the oddly named Museum of Women and Automata in farther-out Neuilly close to the Bois. The 43 bus takes us to yet another limestone *hôtel* built around a central court. It is smaller, newer, less grand than the great counterparts that house the Rodin and Picasso museums. But the foyer is marbly and cool, and the museum manager who sells us tickets assures us that the automata will indeed be set in motion at 3 P.M. ten minutes hence. We wait with a gaggle of young Americans and a few miscellaneous, French-speaking others.
>
> At three we are herded into the first of several rooms filled with such wonders as a letter from Mme. Curie, a flashy oil of a Liberian black woman turning into an orchid, a society portrait of Madame Somebody in a spangled black gown by a painter who also frescoed one of the railway stations, photos of Arletty and Josephine Baker, a bronze cast of Katherine Dunham's handsome feet, a caricature of Brigitte Bardot with sooty eyes and a shelflike *poitrine*, a Mona Lisa postcard endowed with a mustache by Salvador Dali. The central attraction of the first *salle* is a fat, plastery-looking sculpture of a mother and child, larger than life size; of the second, the aptly named *chambre des martyres*, a dramatically lighted glass case enshrining *la corselette de la Reine Marie Antoinette*. Everyone, our guide assures us, marvels at two things: its excellent state of preservation—it is indeed as pretty a morsel of blue taffeta and lace as I've ever seen, although we are given no reason to believe in its authenticity—and its fifty-one centimeter (about twenty inches) waist. George Eliot, in daguerrotype, also

figures among the martyrs, "because, you see, it was very difficult for a woman to be a writer in her time."

In between the large rooms are small passageways with glass cases on each side. Gloves, high-heeled shoes, and shawls diaphanous or embroidered haunt these vitrines, to such an extent that it is a relief to be ushered into the theater of the automata, a large room with several rows of benches and an extravagantly rococo decor made out of a mosaic of common seashells—clam, cowrie, blue mussels jutting outward from its columns like layered razor blades.

The automata, about forty of the total collection of sixty, inhabit a kind of altar draped with red velvet and lighted from below, so that their doll faces are even more eerily distorted. One by one, with the kind of nonstop patter that might accompany a circus act, the guide sets them in motion. First there is a turbaned snake charmer, so marvelously articulated you can see his chest move in and out and his eyebrows up and down as he breathes into his flute while the snake sluggishly winds itself about his neck and forearm. Then come music hall *artistes* with angular chalk-white faces; a variety of doll-women ironing, churning butter, disporting themselves on diminutive swings. A whole village in a glass box twirls. A bumpkin in a soft hat and green pants gets taller, then shorter, as the temperature ostensibly rises and falls. The air is becoming saturated with moted dust, mold, discordant tinkling, a whiff of rancid oiled metal. Stage right, a big doll-woman has been occupied for some time lifting three upended flower pots one after another, finding under each one the grinning face of a monkey.

"Now they have to rest," says the ringmaster, to my vast relief, "and soon they are taking their summer vacation."

We are set loose to wander among the other odd relics. What are we to make of this hodgepodge? Is it misogyny? Fetishism? A naiveté already anachronistic when the *hôtel* was built in 1900? Or perhaps the pathos of some of its unfamous donors, women who could imagine being remembered, if at all, only for their long red gloves, their size three slippers?

I wanted to dismiss the Museum of Women and Automata as camp, as the magpie-like accumulation of a rich suburban lunatic. But it wouldn't go away so easily. What gave the game away, what provoked my visceral rage and shame, was the marzipan ma–donna in the first room. Women, the museum said unequivocally, *are* automata, their faces beatifically painted, their occult insides crammed with intricate and delicate machinery programmed to perform just one marvelous trick over and over, turning out baby after baby until it breaks or wears out.

Why, then, didn't somebody shut this travesty down? Was it so hog-tied by the terms of an impossible bequest that it couldn't be changed, couldn't at least manage a token nod in the direction of women as world leaders, women as scholars, women as athletes, ditch-diggers, brain surgeons, and yes, even *authors*? Both immediately and on reflection, the oddest thing of all about the museum was that it didn't seem to know how odd it was; apparently only my husband and I doubted that more than half of the human race could be fairly represented, with seeming sincerity of intent, by nothing more than a few items of lingerie and some bad art. The group of young Americans touring the museum with us had responded with wide eyes and muted exclamations of wonder and delight to the collections, as to a miniaturized and specialized Disneyland; on leaving, they added their flattering comments to the pile of loose sheets on a small table in the foyer that served as the museum's guest book. Bernard and I both added *un*-flattering comments. Mine, in French, referred to *ce faux musée fétéchiste*. Bernard's went straight to the point: "You've got to be kidding!"

I wrote in French, I think, as a form of denial. For in my own language, and twenty-five years into my own career, I was seized by the horrible conviction that NOTHING HAD CHANGED. Nagging worries rushed back into my mind: why was it that whenever I taught, more than half of my students were women, but when I picked up a literary journal (almost any literary journal) most of its contents were by men? Why did women doctors I knew settle for family practice, women managers murmur about a "glass ceiling" within their companies? Was it possible that I, an ex-newspaper brat, often relished the slaphappy *San Francisco Chronicle* but read *The New York Times* (despite the recent addition of several conspicuously bylined women) with reluctance because the latter appeared to be written of, by, and for men in pinstriped suits? At best, it seemed to me, women writers now had two unsatisfactory options instead of one. For if they wrote as women of women's concerns, they were still subsidiary, specialized, and marginal. And if they adopted, as many ambitious women all too readily do, the values and concerns of a male-dominated society, they ran the risk of betraying—indeed, of never realizing the existence of—many essential parts of themselves.

We need to be reminded what some of these mostly male values are, for they are so pervasive, so taken for granted, that it can be hard to see, in our everyday lives, what they are and how they operate. A man's life—I am speaking in the largest of generalities and on a millennial scale about men who are mostly Western and white—is founded on certain assumptions: the value of strength, physical or mental; the primacy of the striving individual; the importance of competition; the need to acquire and maintain territory of all kinds; the desire to be "the best," which in turn mandates the establishment and maintenance of hierarchies. Men also have believed that truth is objective, or at least knowable, and that once decided upon, it ought to be imposed upon others, a conviction that has led inexorably to wars of territory, religion, and ideology, and to much of the avoidable suffering and slaughter that constitute the greater part of what men have collectively agreed to call history.

Women and children—who constitute together the vast majority of the world's populations—have until the most recent times been crucially subsumed under man's territorial imperative; and all of women's manifold works are still radically trivialized by man's hierarchies. It is worth noting that the ancient arts of women, the arts of weaving, sewing, basketry, pottery, are customarily not even regarded as arts, but dismissed as crafts, their magnificent makers, largely anonymous until this century, treated as anthropological curiosities. Literature, a "fine art," would seem to be a major exception to this dismissal, yet even here the divas of our small pantheon are praised for their genius, derided because they are few. I have used the word "diva" with malice aforethought, for a diva is literally a goddess, hence an exception, with little to do with the ordinary lives of women. Elevated by exclusion, she remains a curiosity, and need not be taken seriously.

But there is no denying that the strength, courage, and initiative we associate with male values can be not only admirable but essential to the survival of ideas as well as people. And competitiveness may be hard-wired into both halves of the human species, for a self-conscious—which is to say a human—self makes comparisons and wants to feel superior to whatever it sees as "other." Further, the ethic of competition and conquest, only a little sublimated, has been the mighty engine driving many achievements in science, philosophy, the arts.

But we live now in a vastly overcrowded world that is running out of everything, even water and air and, most crucially, *time*—time in which to react and restore, lest the planet die and with it the magnificent web of interrelated species, that, as a late afterthought, includes our own. In such a world, war is obsolete, economic "growth" an ongoing environmental catastrophe, cooperation and altruism emerging global imperatives. We can no longer assume that the political and economic institutions we take for granted will still make sense in a century, or even a generation, when their effects are already so mixed. A crucial example: multinational corporations, with revenues larger than those of most countries, may be the most powerful structures in the contemporary world. They waste resources and exploit people. Yet their dubious activities and products have brought unlikely chunks of the world into communication and established interdependencies that may yet force the world toward unity. But corporations are not about communication and interdependence, but about property and profit; does it follow that these concepts, too, may be obsolete? Most radical of all, the cherished notion of "the individual" may have seen its best days. For whatever its degree of differentiation, no organism, from the least cell of a coral reef to, say, a Stephen Hawking, can flourish without the efforts of countless others, nor is a truly constructive world order conceivable that does not bear this truth constantly in mind.

The large virtues of cooperation, empathy, altruism and the smaller ones of conciliation, thrift, and making-do have traditionally been associated with women, and have been inextricably bound up with the very biology that until quite recently has cruelly hampered women's achievements in other fields of endeavor, writing among them. Educated, "liberated" American women, free—although that freedom is now under siege—to choose their own reproductive destinies, tend to forget how terrible the exactions of women's biological endowment can be, how total is their unmitigated sway over the lives of the overwhelming majority of the world's women.

Claire Tomalin's *The Life and Death of Mary Wollstonecraft*, one of the books that mattered intensely to me during the sixties and seventies, one of several that I reread after our return from Paris, offers a poignant instance of the clash between women as doers, dreamers, and makers, and Woman as biological automaton. Here is Tomalin's account of Wollstonecraft's death from septicemia, eleven days after the birth of the infant who would grow up to be Mary Shelley:

> On Wednesday night she rallied slightly again; on Thursday evening Carlisle warned them to expect her death soon, but still she lived for the whole of Friday and Saturday. Godwin's friends sat dishevelled about the house, eager to go on helpful errands, whilst the terrible slow process dragged on. She was no longer coherent in her expressions, but tried to do as she was told, attempting to sleep for instance, though she could not do more than feign the breathing of a sleeping person for a minute or two. She asked her nurses not to bully her, she did not mention religion apart from one exclamation: "Oh, Godwin, I am in heaven," to which he is supposed to have answered anxiously, "You mean, my dear, that your symptoms are a little easier. . . ."
> The shivering fits had ceased after Thursday. On Sunday night Carlisle told Godwin to go to bed, at six in the morning he called him, and at twenty to eight she died. "She had died a death," as one respectable clergyman was soon to remark, "that strongly marked the distinction of the sexes, by pointing out the destiny of woman, and the diseases to which they were peculiarly liable." [1]

Wollstonecraft, author of *A Vindication of the Rights of Woman*, already had a three-year-old daughter, Fanny, by her disastrously romantic liaison with the seducer Gilbert Imlay, an adventure in which biology overrode feminist principle. William Godwin famously opposed marriage on philosophical grounds, as did Mary. Their prickly courtship was further complicated by Godwin's interests in other women. Both remained ambivalent about marriage, but marry they did, on March 29, 1797, early in the pregnancy that was to lead to Mary's death. During their five months of marriage, Godwin wrote in a separate house nearby; in the course of the working day, he and Wollstonecraft sent frequent notes to each other. Easily delivered of her first child, Wollstonecraft had expected no difficulty giving birth to the second. At the time of her agonizing death, she was just thirty-eight years old.

Here is Simone de Beauvoir on the "destiny" that destroyed Mary Wollstonecraft. "Destiny" is also the title of the first part of the first book of *The Second Sex*. In its landmark first chapter, de Beauvoir characterizes the destiny of *all* female mammals, among them *femina sapiens scribens*: ". . . though the female plays a fundamentally active role in procreation, she *submits* to the coition, which invades her individuality and introduces an alien element through penetration and internal fertilization." Pregnancy furthers the process:

> First violated, the female is then alienated—she becomes, in part, another than herself. . . . Tenanted by another, who battens upon her substance throughout the period of pregnancy, the female is at once herself and other than herself; and after the birth she feeds the newborn upon the milk of her breasts. . . . The male is thus permitted to express himself freely; the energy of the species is well integrated into his own living activity. On the contrary, the individuality of the female is opposed by the interest of the species; it is as if she were possessed by foreign forces—alienated. . . . Woman, like man, *is* her body; but her body is something other than herself.[2]

No writer has better described the enormity of female biology. Hundreds of times in each woman's life, she is visited by the power to *make another human being*, another life to be lived and realized. Her body is the vestibule between the worlds of spirit and matter, the theater in which the weird drama of incarnation plays itself out. Whether or not she chooses the difficult path of reconciling her single, striving self—a self endowed by society with goals and a will modeled after the male—with the demands of the species, no woman who has fully understood this power can ever take lightly any manifestation of life.

It is a paradox that, in a world now fatally at odds with itself, it is the historical "alienation" of woman through forced child-bearing and rearing that has evoked in her the qualities the world most needs. Childbirth is the moral antithesis of war; and lactation, with its loving concentration and transmission of substance, provides both metaphor and model for the cherishing of resources that may yet save the planet and all its creatures. No woman who has made, or thought of making, a new life cell by cell from the substance of her own body and spirit, should be able to countenance the expenditure of that life and countless others so that a politician may "stand tall," the continued waste of natural resources be "defended," or an ideologue of a different stripe be toppled from power.

In this world view, a view that begins in the fragile splendor of possibility that each living thing briefly embodies, war is—I repeat—obsolete, history a lethal myth, mindless competition a luxury the earth can no longer afford. Power, once seized, rebounds against powerful and powerless alike. It feeds on inequity of every kind, but most of all on the calamitously unjust concentration of resources in the hands of an overweening few. If the earth's remaining resources—I am speculating, remember, on a global and millennial scale, though the years remaining to life on this planet may be far fewer—were shared and cherished, power as we have known it historically might eventually wither away. But close up and in the finite meantime, "the best" remains the enemy of the good, since it can keep us from stitching up those useful patchworks of partial helps that might cover many of world society's gaping needs.

What conclusions can be drawn from these musings? The first is that conclusions are beside the point; women, creatures of flux and making, may incline more easily to find truth in process. But neither women nor men can any longer afford to live as automata on a threatened planet, still locked in the mechanical repetition of old roles, old assumptions that are worn out and infinitely destructive. Both need to feel as clearly as they think, to question freely, to accept the limitations of personal freedom and property that may be inevitable because we have already squandered so much. We can scarcely begin to imagine what sort of world might evolve from a female ethic of mercy, saving, and sharing, and it would be fatuous to assume that even a world view founded on the ethos of female biology would be without its own kinds of privation, suffering, even violence.

The process, itself a moral stance, that may suggest itself to authors who happen to be female is a familiar, ongoing one: to observe, to question, to ponder, to shape, to speak. Perhaps some hint and hope for the future may be found in the last lines of Adrienne Rich's visionary long poem "Transcendental Etude" (1977):

> Vision begins to happen in such a life
> as if a woman quietly walked away

from the argument and jargon in a room
and sitting down in the kitchen, began turning in her lap
bits of yarn, calico and velvet scraps,
laying them out absently on the scrubbed boards
in the lamplight, with small rainbow-colored shells
sent in cotton-wool from somewhere far away,
and skeins of milkweed from the nearest meadow—
original domestic silk, the finest findings—
and the darkblue petal of the petunia,
and the dry darkbrown lace of seaweed;
not forgotten either, the shed silver
whisker of the cat,
the spiral of paper-wasp-nest curling
beside the finch's yellow feather.
Such a composition has nothing to do with eternity,
the striving for greatness, brilliance—
only with the musing of a mind
one with her body, experienced fingers quietly pushing
dark against bright, silk against roughness,
pulling the tenets of a life together
with no mere will to mastery,
only care for the many-lived, unending
forms in which she finds herself,
becoming now the sherd of broken glass
slicing light in a corner, dangerous
to flesh, now the plentiful, soft leaf
that wrapped round the throbbing finger, soothes the wound;
and now the stone foundation, rockshelf further
forming underneath everything that grows.[3]

NOTES

1. Claire Tomalin, *The Life and Death of Mary Wollstonecraft* (New York: Mentor Books/The New American Library, 1976), p. 220.

2. Simone de Beauvoir, *The Second Sex* (New York: Bantam Books, 1953), pp. 19-26.

3. Adrienne Rich, *The Fact of a Doorframe: Poems Selected and New, 1950-1984* (New York: W. W. Norton & Co., 1984), pp. 268-69. Quoted with permission of the publisher.

DARK TURTLES AND BRIGHT TURTLES

Brenda Hillman

Was just walking in the dry wilderness trying to think about whether I have anything to say about tradition. Hot, hot, dry day, brushfires still raging over in Calaveras County, making the slightest breeze a more serious matter. The Republican convention is just over; women were given freedom, room to speak, as in Marilyn Quayle wearing her red, white, and blue suit talking about "women's nature." Overhead, in the buckeye, the whir of redwing blackbirds, and I stop at the place we call Jewel Lake.

Sometimes the image is tossed up just when we need it: today, there is a log with seven bright turtles facing the sun. They are all lined up. If they were a little deeper, they would be World War I helmets. I'm thinking about tradition watching them, and then, suddenly, the image completes itself.

I look to the left, and see another log. It is in the shade, not the sun. There are turtles on it, too, many of them, but instead of being lined up and sunny like the other turtles, they're piled on each other, scrambling, disordered. I can't help wondering if they're having fun, climbing up on each other's heads and backs to see better. . . I take the metaphoric value of the scene to be that there are at least two traditions, and probably each writer is like a pond, able to hold them both at the same time.

*

I never felt "held back" as a poet because of my gender, either as a student or when I began to publish. At the same time: the entire course of my life and art have been shaped by a struggle I have perceived to be and have internalized as an existential one.

Most of the struggle for me to write anything at all—poems, letters, essays, lists, journal entries—has had to do with being female, the sense that to be female is a metaphor for existence itself. Consequently, identity, existence, nonexistence, and the awakening of the soul became the subjects of my art.

I'm interested in boundary conditions, both in the self and in the universe. I've been reading a lot about what scientists call "event horizons" at the edges of black holes. It turns out they don't know what happens at the edge of black holes and how the light goes in and stays out at the same time. I like their examples: "If a scout were sent out by the captain to explore a black hole. . . ," and although I don't hold onto the technical details, I am fascinated by the notion of these boundaries in which things become what they are not, and hover there. It seems interesting to consider this in relation to women's writing, especially those acts of positively charged darkness. To be female and to write is to search out—and make the best of—what loves us despite abandonment, despite what disappears.

*

I find myself reading the work of many courageous contemporaries, those who address the fears and the problems of being female and conscious. As we do more of the work of criticism ourselves, we must not neglect women. The first wave has passed, and the second wave, and the backlash has given way to a deadening ignorance. We need to understand our inadmissable fears and jealousies—not only of what has been denied to us by the fears of men, but also what we continue to deny each other. It's serious. We are not doing enough for each other because we are still afraid. A friend of mine says she refuses to be in an anthology of women poets. She does not want to be called a woman poet. This position is poisonous, I tell her. She is afraid—that tired old argument—that it sets up a separate standard for her. But here's the problem: I got a new literary magazine in the mail and only *two* of the eighteen writers in it are women. The problem is that when I teach at a writers' conference, when I teach graduate students, three-quarters of the students are women. Yet even many publications with female editors do not give equal space to the writing of women. And the problem is that one of my favorite writers (a great big traditional writer) says he dislikes Emily Dickinson and in general does not like the work of women because he hates "subjective verse." So it could be that women writers may still need to give each other special attention, to develop enough self-nurturing that we can see the task ahead of us.

*

I was thinking about double traditions and the body, rereading Sappho to teach to the Greek Thought class, thinking of how very, very much one can say in three-line fragments. My daughter walks in, who, at completely wonderful thirteen, makes me whisper to myself at least once a day, "*Something* is going well, she's turning out to be an original." I love the way genetics and tradition fool us into thinking we can make predictions. Her close-together hips and her creamy skin are like nothing on either side of the family; where did the very full, slightly pouty, curled-up lip come from? In the same way, the young body of a new poetry develops. . . .

*

In order to explore my spiritual and creative ancestry, I began studying the Gnostic traditions. The Gnostics hold that inner knowledge is divine, is on fire, and that our job is to get through a great deal of external suffering to be reunited with our true selves. Each time an individual comes into awareness, it is a cosmic occurrence. I've been interested in the nonhierarchical, fantastic, and magical aspects of these ancient sects, not just in the central emphasis on self-knowledge, and I've found that, more than other Western esoteric traditions, Gnosticism has been quite compatible with feminist awareness and poetry. The type of self-knowledge that leads us "forward" is not the easy kind; it is complex and full of suffering, and is, in some ways, deeply incompatible with a culture that asks you to show results for the work you are doing. So often, there are no results. There are many rich, yielding inner darknesses as well as inner lights.

In the service of the searching, confused soul—as we begin to write toward it—we will never solve, capture, or meet the "you" really, but as it goes around corners we keep catching glimmerings of it. Our contemporary "soul-in-motion" may be too hyperactive and outdoorsy for pure Gnostics, but I think of it as a Gnostic quest anyway, and it is certainly a feminist quest, and I know I am making up a tradition as I go along.

*

The question of tradition cannot be addressed without addressing the question of audience. In a recent essay on the subject of audience called "Tack Hammer to the Crazy Bone," Sandra Alcosser writes: "Do not imagine me. Let me come close to you. Of course, there is a wish for connection, but to be aware of my reader would cause me to fight against my own desire to please. . . . To know my reader is to court a lover, a censor, a shadow, a mirror, is to manipulate both myself and the other."[1]

*

But still. I'm fed, intimidated by, and inspired by the male canon, imagining the writers in it to be like those columns we had to memorize in the architecture segment (doodles: curlicues and fat lilies all over the margins) of Art History: Doric, Corinthian, Ionic, holding up their huge imaginary building. Tradition is mostly an imaginary construct: Hopkins, Yeats, Eliot, Lowell—all columns in the mind. We can lift this imaginary building and rearrange it. I'm put off by the idea of "greatness," and prefer to think that each reader walks in each day and invents her set of immortals, that the set changes. I find myself increasingly drawn to the use of "unknown" writers when I teach; I like to juxtapose poems by students with those by famous dead people, because making meaning is an act of endless invention by individuals. There are many things we can do to expand tradition: teach poems by writers of color, teach poems of many different styles and by both genders. People ask me what to read; I say, "Read what will comfort you. And after that, read what upsets you. Read what will make you grow."

I am also interested in what is stylistically experimental in women's writing: fragmentation, hesitations, interruption, secret singing, the nonlinear—what is at the edge (the inner edge) of our voices since Sappho.

The trick is to discover how far out on the branch you can go and still "make sense." I love many of the nonrepresentational language experiments, though some of the poets regard "making sense" as suspect. Most often I find myself called to a poetry that says a thing strangely, and that has a thing to say. I am drawn to risk in poetry, but only if it is accompanied by resonant emotional content. Which is a way of saying, we have to use our hearts and our heads.

*

Finally, an excerpt from one of the Gnostic texts called "The Thunder: Perfect Mind." Probably written in the second century by a woman, it expresses great power in contradiction:

> I am the one who has been hated everywhere
>   and who has been loved everywhere.
> I am the one whom they call Life
>   and you have called Death. . .
> I am the one whom you have scattered
>   and you have gathered me together.
> I am the one before whom you have been ashamed
>   and you have been shameless to me.
> I am she who does not keep festival
>   and she whose festivals are many.
> I, I am godless
>   and I am the one whose God is great. . .
> I am unlearned
>   and they learn from me. . . .[2]

NOTES

1. Sandra Alcosser, "Tack Hammer to the Crazy Bone," in "For Whom Does the Poet Write? Twenty American Poets Respond to Fred Chappell,"

Manoa, A Pacific Journal of International Writing, Vol. 3, No. 1 (Spring 1991), pp. 78-79, © U. of Hawaii Press, 1991.

2. James Robinson, ed., *The Nag Hammadi Library* (San Francisco: Harper Collins, 1990), p. 297.

ROBERT JIMMY ALLEN

Judith Kitchen

When I was five, my name was Robert Jimmy Allen. It was a name I chose carefully, taking it from my three favorite boys. Every morning I rode in from my home in the country to kindergarten with Mrs. Davenport, the third grade teacher. At 11:30, I spent half an hour sitting in the small desk next to hers until the class was dismissed and she could drive me home. For thirty minutes, I listened, watched, and secretly learned to read and do arithmetic. I kept my eyes open. I saw Robert, Jimmy, and Allen.

I was five and I lived in the country without many playmates. My father was a physicist, a socialist, an atheist—not in any given order. He believed I could do anything. It did not occur to him that my sex was a limitation. It did not occur to me. He built me a pulley so that I could haul utensils up to my sandbox on the top of the chicken coop. He let me climb trees and swing higher than I ought to until the whole metal frame lifted in the ground, shuddered.

When I came home from kindergarten, I announced that, from then on, I would answer only to my new name. For several months, I became someone else.

I now realize I was learning to read in several ways. Learning to read the society, the systems already in place, the language of power. But I was also learning to read myself—and what I found there was the desire for new (vicarious) experience. I chose Robert Jimmy Allen. He was my first experience of entering a story, of literature.

Looking back, I do not see him as symptomatic of something amiss. I do not regret that I did not choose a female name. I do not think it was from lack of role models that my eyes lit on those three boys. Their collective life seemed possible to me. I tried it on. It fit.

I am ten. I own the highest spot in the tree. It is mine by right of courage. No one else can climb that high. I look down on the backyard world of childhood. My mother ventures into it only to call us in from baseball games, cowboys and Indians, neighborhood intrigue. She does not know about the secret-compartment rings, the furtive forays across the forbidden railroad tracks; the time we lost Joel Sundquist's father's hammer. She calls us in to dinner.

Her voice comes now, clear and distinct. I do not know what it meant to me. The tree was so tall I could lose myself in the branches. I could refuse to answer, watch her move small below me, shading her eyes, peering up.

There is a time in a girl's life when she is most masculine, when she feels power in her body, a sense of flight. It is so fleeting, she almost misses it. Turn around once in your strawberry dress and it's gone. If I were another kind of feminist, I'd like to think that was the time she was most feminine, but part of me knows that's not true. Something happens to the body. I don't want to deny the physical. Being female is not, it seems to me, a construction: it's a fact. It comes with blood and fluctuating hormones and birth and much much more. It's a state of being as well as a state of mind. What I hid from, at the top of the maple tree, was the world I would climb down to—the woman I would inevitably become.

By fifteen, I liked the feel of my corduroy skirt swirling up around bare legs. I liked the feeling of being center stage, all eyes on us. "Joe Strzepek, he's our man, if he can't do it—Blencoe can." Each cheerleader in turn, whirl and kick and, at the end, a soaring, back arched, body launched into air. I didn't have to tell myself to like this. I simply did.

I also liked to sit on the hot-air register, reading. This was a secret vice, one I kept to myself. I picked my authors carefully, reading everything the local library had on the shelf. This was the year I read Hemingway, Fitzgerald, Faulkner. They were mine—every glittering flapper, every tough-skinned soldier, every trapped confederate. I took them so wholly into myself that I could feel them move, like a kicking fetus.

If I identified with any character, it was an identification removed from my experience of the world. These books *were* my experience of the world. They took me out of myself. Caddy—her very absence set the heart in motion. I *was* Caddy, haunted by her moment in the tree, by what she had seen. With her, I slid down the drainpipe and out and away, opening the rich field of imagination.

I hoarded the heat. Everyone complained. (Come set the table. Why don't you clean your room?) I did not talk about what I had come to understand. I brushed out my pincurls, found my red lipstick, slipped into my blue and white jacket, ready for the game.

I search my early years for clues to how I became myself. What I see is fairly ordinary. As in all stories, there are places where my experience is unique.

My father, for one thing. I do know that his message was always one of equality. He was more interested in what I was thinking than how I was looking. I don't remember him telling me I looked pretty. (I want to be called beautiful.) I do remember his pride when I'd argue with him.

My mother, for another. It seems to me now that she was a bright, frustrated woman. There was more in her than her circumstances would allow. She had worked her way through both high school and college. Education was her passion. (Next to cleanliness.) She was a good, kind woman. My sophomore year, she took in a girl in the senior class. Pat was the eighth of twelve children, told by her mother to quit school and find a job. For that year, my mother nurtured someone who must have seemed to her more like herself than her own daughter was. She sent Pat off to college and, for twenty-five years, Pat has been a first-grade teacher: my mother's legacy.

My teachers. For the most part widows or spinsters—and tough. They always acted as though I would, as a matter of course, perform for them. Write the stories. Decline the nouns. Do them proud. They never once gave me the impression that, because I was a girl, l was lost.

Professor Munford's back was straighter than that of any of his precious Puritans. A spare man, tall, uncomfortable. He had two pairs of glasses and he absent-mindedly changed them as he switched from talking to us to reading from the poems. Every once in a while he was in transition and his blue eyes went glassy, squinting as though there were something out there yet to come clear.

There was. We were, as a class, coming to terms with what it meant to read a poem. He was open, generous, took our work seriously. He divided the class into four groups and assigned us each a poem. We could write one page only. His most frequent comment was, "Is this the word you mean?" Often he read to us from the work of some former student. I wanted to be in that pile— the pile of papers he might someday want to quote. He was opening up a whole new world. Once again, it did not occur to me it was not mine for the taking.

In my senior year of college I married, changed my major from mathematics to American Literature, learned to budget and cook, directed two plays, discovered just how much I loved poetry. In 1963, we were reading not only Williams, Frost, and Stevens, but Delmore Schwartz, Theodore Roethke, John Berryman, Robert Lowell, Elizabeth Bishop. "Too bad," my beloved professor told me, "you have such good ideas but no vehicle for expressing them." Possibly this was my first encounter with the male academic standard. Possibly I was just what he claimed—a bad writer, one who could not communicate what she intuitively knew about the poem. I only know that desire is more than dream. With a physical intensity, I wanted to be able to speak about the poems I loved. I wanted to make them come clear for someone else.

Today, I believe, Howard Munford would have spoken to me about graduate school. Would have encouraged me. But I was married (too bad) and my fate was summarily sealed. I spent the next eight years working while my husband studied. I had babies. After that, we went to Brazil. I lost the young woman who loved poetry. She receded so successfully I forgot she was there. She was buried in womanly concerns—real concerns—food and laundry and the occasional pleasure.

Today, I believe, we would deplore the circumstances that led that young woman to put aside her own desires. But I was wholly complicitous. It never occurred to me. It never occurred to my husband. It didn't occur to my erudite professor, my socialist father, my passionate mother. Quite honestly, it didn't occur to the society at large. I had two babies in diapers when Gloria Steinem hit the newsstands. We were the same age, but on opposite sides of the cusp. I had married early, rushed into a world that was waiting to buoy me along. The other world was on hold—and I had no idea how to get back to it.

All semester I rode my bicycle to campus to take a class while my youngest son was in kindergarten. This time I brought to it not only love, but a kind of hard-earned knowledge. I knew what it meant to reach for the ineffable. My final paper looked at the use of poetry in the plays of T. S. Eliot, Archibald MacLeish, and Harold Pinter. I concentrated on moments when the pressure of emotion forced the language to reach for poetry, when nothing else would do. I concluded that the poet-turned-playwright does not demonstrate this kind of internal necessity as much as the playwright tugged, only half willingly, into verse. Professor Kinnamon took me aside after the last class. "Have you considered getting a Ph.D.?" he asked.

My heart expanded, then settled back, calm for the first time in years. Yes. Until that very moment. And then, with his belief in me, I did not need to get a degree. Could not imagine getting a degree. Could not imagine putting myself at their feet and learning their vocabulary and playing their games.

All those years I was jealous. I wanted to be a part of that academic world, the one where I had felt most myself (most recognizably *a* self). I watched my husband go off each day and it seemed to me that my turn would never come. It looked so easy. He'd walk out the door (two tiny heads in the window), turn and wave, then off he'd go, his head swimming in higher mathematics before he even reached the corner. At night he'd return to us, enter our world. He never once seemed guilty, never turned again to see those two faces needing his.

I like to think that, given the right circumstances, given a different atmosphere and attitude, I could have done the same. But part of me knows that the body would have interceded. The breasts spurted milk when the baby cried. It was out of my control. I was held by invisible threads, and it was not just casual housekeeping that let me lick the bottom of their spoons. They were part of me; I don't believe I could have turned and walked away so easily—and I believe that is part of what it is to be female.

When I read Eliot (I grow old), I believe in a unique sensibility. No one else could say it quite that way. No one else would want to. And my job, it seems to me, is to come as close as I can to being that sensibility—for the duration of the poem. To enter its world. To grow old. The nature of literature is individual. The literary "I" speaks from a self; it opposes community. It is the private, briefly made public through the shared medium of language. This is its very reason for being. And this is the tradition I enter (willingly)— I decide to add my singular voice to the cauldron of voices.

This singularity of experience matters to me. It is what I write from—and for. To that end, there is not male or female art. To that end, if we submit to all-female journals, we make a statement—we say that we have an agenda, that gender comes before art. However much I might like to be a part of that community, I am not. I climb the tree alone. (My mother grows small. The leaf looms large.)

The poets who spoke to me were mostly male. In my case, this was not through lack of female models—though, of course, there were fewer women to read. Dickinson, Moore, Bishop (those precise ladies) spoke *to* me, but not *for* me. In fact, there did not seem to be a poetry of my experience—with the blazing exception of Plath.

And Plath was misread, misrepresentative. She had been usurped by the "cause"—thus severed from those of us who knew her work from the inside, recognized each image as interior. It's taken a long while to win her back, to make her wholly individual.

So I settled for Lowell, for Frost and Stevens and Eliot. (Settled? They gave me life!) So I named my loves, and they were Robert Wallace Thomas. I tried them on. They fit.

Postscript

It would not take much of a deconstructionist to see the holes in my narrative, the places where I suspect I do protest too much. Or much of a feminist theorist to point the finger and say, Aha! Gender shapes us. It shaped me, I can see that. The culture is loud in its silence. Interestingly, through this silence, *because* of this silence, I taught myself to read—and then to write.

When I read, am I reading through the eyes of T. S. Eliot? Adrienne Rich says, "we need to know the writing of the past, and know it differently than we have ever known it, not to pass on a tradition but to break its hold over us." Am I, however inadvertently, passing on the tradition without changing it in the ways that Adrienne Rich insists we must? The answer is the old ambivalent "yes and no." But I am ambivalent about everything—about marriage and motherhood and writing and teaching, so why should this be any different? I feel responsibilities I don't want to feel.

The other day, an adjunct (female) in our English department asked of a newly hired feminist theorist (also female), "How do the feminists feel about Hawthorne?" I was terrified by the answer. Not by what she said (I've already forgotten that), but by the fact that she attempted to answer for all of us. She did not begin her sentence with, "I'm not sure what the 'feminists' think, but here's how I feel." *That* I would have understood. Because *that*, I always thought, was what we were fighting for.

Today, I spend much of my time reading books of poems, selecting from among stacks of new books the ones I will eventually review. In this capacity, I believe that I am helping to shape a tradition for the future. I am adding to it the voices of writers— male *and* female—whose words seem to me to deserve more readers. I must admit that I am aware of myself as a female reviewer. I admit that I feel (subtly) some pressure to be especially aware of the work of women and other minorities. I also admit that I may be hard on the work of women—if the images feel familiar (and they do, they do), then I want the writer to go beyond the *fact* of her femininity. I want to see the world through *her* eyes, not through some programmatic prescription. Such writing limits its possibilities in advance. If there is a "female" way of reading, it must be rooted in individual experience, individual imagination, ultimately in the individual body. And it must be accessible to other imaginations—potentially *all* others—as theirs must be to mine. If there is, indeed, something like a male tradition, then we need a female tradition which will be open to men, which will teach them to read as we do. I realize now that what I want is a wider tradition, not a different one. I don't want to set up the same old polarities, but to reconcile differences through understanding. This must be what the imagination is all about. Otherwise, why read? Why write? So I resist you, Adrienne Rich. I will not be pulled into your trap, either. Because you, like Eliot, seem to be talking from *outside* the poem—and I want to come from inside. I want to be in that readerly place where gender is inconsequential.

BREAKING THE MOLD

Maxine Kumin

In the late fifties, when Anne Sexton and I, two suburban house-wives, were learning our trade, we had no female mentors. In truth, there were none on our then-limited horizon. No women's studies programs, no rosters of readings and residencies with wo-men well—or even ill—represented. The poets we had adored in our teens—Millay and Teasdale and Elinor Wylie—whose splen-did sonnets and tight quatrains and ballads of love and unrequital we had secretly emulated, languished for the most part unread or scorned. Even H. D., who had once been romantically linked to Ezra Pound, hardly existed for the poets of the fifties; certainly no one at that time was academically engaged in analyzing her mythic bent.

In the university, contemporary poetry texts, all but womanless to the best of my recollection, seldom went beyond World War I. To anthologists Wilfred Owen seemed a useful cutoff point. While Sanders and Nelson's *Chief Modern Poets of England and America*, published by Macmillan in 1943 and widely used in academe, did contain sizable excerpts from the work of Millay and Wylie, Marianne Moore, for example, was absent. And the presence of some poetry by women in a college text did not guarantee their representation in the lectures or classroom discussion. I recall a course with Robert Hillyer that opened with Robert Bridges and ended with Kenneth Fearing. Yeats and Eliot were its twin pillars of intellect. Nowhere in my notes can I uncover a woman poet praised or disparaged—female bards obviously did not matter.

Not once during my Radcliffe undergraduate years (1942-46) did I find a female instructor, assistant, associate, or, heaven for-fend, full professor in any discipline. True, Maud Cam reigned in astronomy at Harvard, the exception that proved the rule. And in my junior year I did meet one woman section leader of a history course.

By the late fifties, Marianne Moore had become the Maud Cam of American poetry. She had won the National Book Award, the Bollingen, and the Pulitzer. When in 1953 she was praised by Robert Lowell as "the best woman poet in English," Langston Hughes flung back his quick-witted riposte: "I consider her the most famous Negro woman poet in America." But even as we chuckle at the rejoinder, we can see the double standard at work, a standard that prevailed throughout the fifties and sixties.

However much we might admire Marianne Moore's encyclopedic miniatures, they did not provide Sexton and me with a workable model. The picture of her as a rather more complicated figure—self-effacing maiden and suffragette, pixie innovator of eccentric new prosodies, antimilitarist—was yet to emerge. We travelled to Wellesley College to hear her read her poems, a scene I have described in the foreword to *Marianne Moore: The Art of a Modernist*: We "sat in the balcony and could barely see the delicate face of the poet, so modestly did she incline her head over the page. Even amplified she was extremely hard to hear. We sat on the edge of our seats and strained for every word, following along in her books wherever we could do so. Afterward, we were too shy to join the group clustered around her. It was enough to know we had been in the presence of a poetic genius, even—or especially?—one who read badly."[1]

Much lionized but little read—all her books went out of print in her lifetime—Moore has now, with the flowering of feminist literary history, been accorded her due. Elizabeth Bishop, the subject of recent extensive critical attention, was not widely noticed in the fifties. She spent most of that decade in Brazil. Once settled in Boston, her enduring literary friendships, except for her association with Moore, who had been her mentor, were with men.

Paradoxically, despite her pre-eminent friendship with Robert Lowell, the new "confessional" strain in poetry alarmed her. She was a profoundly private person. Matters of gender, it seemed, were off-limits in her work. Indeed, later, when such collections entered the canon in the early seventies, Bishop refused requests to reprint her poems in exclusively female anthologies. And thus, despite the fact that we lived in the same environs, neither Sexton nor I ever came to know Bishop. I did encounter her in the late sixties or early seventies, if memory serves correctly, at one of the Harvard houses, where I was to give a postprandial reading. We were seated together. I was visibly nervous; the utensils shook in my hand. But to my delight, when Miss Bishop spoke to me it was about her goats, and how painful it had been to leave them behind in Brazil. I seem to remember some snapshots of goats and several stories about their versatility and wit. Not one word about poetry passed our lips.

Louise Bogan, whom Sexton and I had met briefly at the MacDowell Colony through our poetry workshop leader, John Holmes—this would have been 1959 or 60—had already spoken, saying women have no wilderness in them ("they are provident instead"). We sat on the cot in her studio in Peterborough and sipped jasmine tea she brewed on a hot plate. We longed to attain her stature as a poet, but it seemed we would never acquire what we read as her self-assurance and deftness. Sexton's cup clattered in the saucer; we were always being betrayed in some way by our nervous awe.

Years later, when Ecco Press reprinted the long-lapsed *Blue Estuaries* and *Journey around My Room*, I came to appreciate Bogan and to rue the fact that she had seemed so formidable, so distant.

It seemed, with these signal exceptions, that all the lean, hard, muscular poetry was being written by men. What was left was verse devoted to God, butterflies, and brownies, composed by the little three-name Letitia ladies. With this epithet we set ourselves apart, guilty of envy and snobbism in equal measure.

I do not mean to suggest that our artistic commitment had anything to do with feminist issues. We were far too naive for that, and far too harassed on the home front with toddlers and first-graders, laundry and dishes. The women's movement was still some years in the future. But we made, willynilly, the connection between gender and success. In an era when even a sympathetic editor would not print a poem written by a woman more than once every few issues, there was etiquette as well as ethic involved in devising ways to get our poems published.

You drive like a man, male poets told you admiringly as you bullied your way through rush-hour traffic to deliver them on time to a prereading dinner party. *You write like a man,* they said, if your genderless new poem rippled with the biceps of active verbs. But the curious thing is that even at that seminal time in our development as writers, this oblique conferring of privilege seemed preposterous to us.

Yes, we wanted to be taken seriously. We wanted to be counted as members of the club. But we could not possibly write like men. Whatever we were—daughters, wives, mothers, lovers—was intensely female. And the impulse for poems came directly out of our female perceptions.

Sexton went on to confront the still-rigid mores of that period with defiant poems about masturbation, abortion, incest, and menstruation that aroused the ire of more than one male reviewer. How quaint their remonstrances seem today! Many of my own tribal poems—poems about family constellations, particularly the mother-daughter bond—evolved out of my personal experience. How could it be otherwise? Gender casts a long shadow and I am happy to shelter in it. I think even my animal poems betray, or perhaps loudly announce, my gender.

Where did the courage come from to break out of the mold? What had changed between the preceding generation and our own? The social historian will have many answers, and any that I might offer seem hedged about with qualifications: World War II and Rosie the Riveter had begun the liberation of women in the workplace. The fifties was a period of consolidation and backtracking, with enormous emphasis on the family. Perhaps new work by women was a reaction to the reimposition of social constraints. We were second-class citizens, the repository of all goodness and truth in the home and seldom welcome outside it. When I was first hired as a part-time English instructor at Tufts University at the end of that decade, I was permitted to teach only freshman composition to the Phys Ed majors and the dental technicians. The loosening in the decades that followed will probably have to wait another twenty years to be fully understood.

I have to say that I love what I am now seeing in poetry written by women, poems full of body language, vivid hetero- and homosexual love poems, intense lyrics of appetite and grief, narrative poems about growing up female in dozens of different ethnics, epics detailing the lives of our least-sung heroines, pioneer wives.

Even from the vantage point of a forty-six-year marriage that has been productive and sustaining, I have to confess to an enormous bias: I will read a woman's words, whether it be fiction, fact, or poetry, before I turn to a parallel work by a man. I am just more interested in, empathic with, the female condition.

We are not a separate race but we possess strong bonds forged by biology and society. Thus I read, admire, and feel reaffirmed by Rich and Levertov, Lord and Van Duyn, by Oles and Olds and Dove, by Toi Derricotte's account of childbirth and Jana Harris's retellings of pioneer women's survivals. I am taken with Ostriker's revisions of the Old Testament fathers and Hacker's spirited French-English rhymings. While many lost women writers are still to be found, I am pleased to see Muriel Rukeyser and Edna Millay, along with H. D., back in print, for if they were not lost to us they were surely misplaced for decades.

Much history remains to be rewritten or reevaluated, but I am old enough now to see how far we have come. When I first began to publish poems in the late fifties, women were still outsiders. They had barely gotten beyond hiding behind a first initial in order to conceal their gender. The good teaching positions and residencies went almost invariably to men, and men were invariably better paid. The ten top editors of literary journals were male, and respected male poets outnumbered women poets ten to one.

In 1993, none of these conditions still obtains. And despite the predictable backlash in these bad economic times, the ratio continues, ever so gradually but inexorably, to be redressed.

The writer Jan Morris, who began life as a man and has continued it as a woman, said once in an essay that in another two hundred years or so, people would "wonder at the primitive nature of our own times, when art could still be collated with gender at all." I disagree. While I too long for a critical standard that is independent of male or female orientation, I feel that gender will always tell. As it should.

NOTES

1. Ed. Joseph Parisi (Ann Arbor: U. of Michigan Press, 1990), pp. viii-ix.

MOSAIC LAW: THE BITS AND PIECES FROM WHICH ONE WOMAN'S POEMS ARE MADE

Cynthia Macdonald

The Eliots are on the bottom shelf at the Brazos Bookstore. Looking for T. S. Eliot's essay on Dante, I discard several volumes of his essays because it isn't in them. I am looking for that essay because I spent a number of months inhabiting the seventh and eighth circles of Dante's Hell, translating those Cantos. Now, I'm writing a short essay on what the process was like. I reach for another Eliot volume and a collection I don't recognize comes to hand. Scanning the index I see: "Silly Novels by Women Novelists." Of course, I think, he's continuing the tradition of attacking women writers, not as Max Beerbohm had in his letter to Virginia Woolf when he said, "Your novels beat me—black and blue. I retire howling, aching, sore. . . I return later. . . No use: I am carried out half-dead. . . ," which at least suggests an awareness that it was the power of women Beerbohm feared, but by dismissing them completely as silly. More bad news about Thomas Stearns Eliot to add to the snips and snippets—good name for a female rock group—which had piled up since the years I had first fallen in love with Eliot and *The Waste Land* at college. I had invested myself so totally in him that our relationship seemed a mutual one. I can, thank goodness, only remember the first lines of my poem that began, "I, too, have crossed the Starnbergersee."

Flipping to the Silly Novelist entry, I begin to read. My God: this isn't Thomas Stearns. It is George. Everything shifts. I had made the stereotyped assumption that only a man would refer to women novelists as silly. The stereotype is part of tradition, not because it is false but because it was, for a time at least, so repetitively true. The stereotype, which also might be called the convention—enables us to move through thinking more rapidly. How can we comfortably exist without it? How can we, poets of either gender, exist with it, we who prize ambiguity and nuance? These questions point to a central difficulty with the "tradition" subject: stereotypes rush in where angels, genderless, fear to tread.

Perhaps I can postpone becoming a fool by delaying the attempt to answer the central question posed in relation to the Eliot essay: how does an ancestral line composed almost entirely of male poets function for me and for other women poets writing today? First, I need to try to answer a question which in my generation necessarily precedes it: why did a little girl born in 1928 wish to become any-thing besides a wife and mother?

Wives in the two worlds inhabited by my family—the New York German Jewish circle of stockbrokers, lawyers, and business-men, and the Southern California circle of the movie industry—did not work. These women were not housewives; there were cooks, maids, nannies, and governesses to attend to *kuchen* and *kinder*. *Küssen* they did themselves when they tucked their children in or before they left for the evening. Many of them did a lot of charity work. My mother—Mummy—didn't; she put in one token day a week. She slept until one in the afternoon unless she was lunching, but she also did less of that than most of her friends. She pursued various ladylike pursuits from time to time, a class in photography or gardening, creating beautiful flower arrangements for the house, reading, doing puzzles.

I don't know how or why she made her choice of amusements, but I believe they had to be amateur pursuits, amateur defined not by whether one was paid for the work—she had paying jobs twice when the family fortunes failed, once doing publicity for the Roxy movie theater and, during the war, working for the Civilian Defense organization—but by a lack of serious investment. My mother's pastimes were actually that. Even the paid jobs had a quality of randomness and passivity about them. Mummy was like a flower floating downstream, bumping into rocks, sticks, or dragonflies. The object in her waterpath would amuse, or confuse her briefly, then the water would carry her on.

Jill Ker Conway, former president of Smith College and writer of the wonderful autobiography, *Road to Corain*, is talking at the

Houston Museum of Fine Arts about her new book, *Written by Herself*. It presents excerpts from autobiographies by twenty-five women. She describes how most of the achieving women—would she call them ladies? she doesn't but that's what they sound like to me—write in the passive voice and describe events as if circumstance or luck is responsible for their accomplishments. She focuses the talk on Jane Addams, who in 1889 founded the first settlement house in the United States. Ms. Ker Conway describes the difference between Addams' account in letters to her sister of the steps she had to take to bring this about—she was both determined and forceful—and the account of it in her autobiography where, describing her much wished-for London visit to Toynbee Hall, the prospective model for a residence she hoped to establish in Chicago, she wrote: "So that it finally came about that in June, 1888. . . I found myself at Toynbee Hall." The sentence almost has the quality of Dorothy landing in Oz. Although she was not at all a floating flower on a stream—we know from a letter to her sister that she had pestered an acquaintance five or six times to arrange the Toynbee Hall visits—she feels the need to present herself as if she were.

Is some of that seeming passivity still necessary for women? Perhaps only for straight women. Most lesbians allow themselves to claim themselves as the makers of their own destiny. Other feminist women wish to, but I believe, in their wish to please men, they often waffle. Pulls and tugs—another rock group?—this subject is more complicated than I want it to be, more complicated than my own progression toward becoming a poet feels to me.

My mother was at a considerable remove from Jane Hull, both chronologically and temperamentally. She never even started to move toward achievement. Yet she had been such a whiz at the Dalton School that she finished all her work by the middle of the year and, so I was told, used to leave the building and go to Central Park to read and play. At Dana Hall she was a vigorous and victorious high jumper, had starred in several plays in male roles, and had made a perfect score in her College Boards in French. She was enough of a rebel at Wellesley to go to a dance in bare legs—which was considered sufficiently shocking to merit the punishment of being confined to the campus at night for the rest of the semester. What happened to her combination of brains and spirit? I don't know. Although I was born only three years after the bare legs episode, I never saw even remnants of the girl I just described. But maybe some of her spirit came through to me, some kind of hidden wish transferred to me.

What about Daddy as a model? In his early thirties he decided he wanted to become a writer, very quickly sold stories to *Colliers* and the *Saturday Evening Post*, then accepted a contract to write movies. As I write this condensed description of those years, I realize it sounds as if I must have caught his spirit, which said, do what you want to do. But it's hard for me to believe that is what happened. He was a removed, bad-tempered figure in my life. I remember telling my governess, Marguerite, that I loved Mummy and hated Daddy. She said, "you can't hate your father," but I knew I often did. One could propose, as I did in relation to Mummy, that some wish in relation to me was transmitted from his unconscious to mine. If so, I believe it was less about writing and more about the exciting world he inhabited because he wrote. The exciting world he was adventurous enough to pursue.

California, 1937. Closed in the house, Cap, our Newfoundland, is bumping the living room window and barking. I'm sitting on the stone terrace with my parents and the six couples who've come for dinner. They're all having drinks. Punctuated by the sound of claws scraping glass and deep woofs, Charlie Brackett, a fellow screenwriter of Daddy's at Metro-Goldwyn Mayer, is describing the new college his daughter attends, a place called Bennington. What he says is fascinating to me: the college closes down in winter and each student gets a job. The job is considered a regular part of the curriculum. "I'm going there," I say when he finishes. I am nine.

The adults smile the way adults often do when a young child makes a pronouncement about his or her future. Perhaps the smile is broader when it breaches class or gender expectations, for example, the child of professionals who says he'll be a fireman, the child of blue collar workers who says she'll be a poet, or the girl who says she'll be a race-car driver or president. I can't remember how broad the smiles were that evening; I can only remember the certainty I felt that Bennington, with its chance for "real" work, was the place for me. Looking back, I believe my announcement that I was going to Bennington is the moment I showed I wanted to be more than "just" a wife and mother.

In those California years, before my parents divorced—Daddy stayed on the West Coast, Mummy and I returned to the East—a great deal of the brief time the three of us were together was spent on tests of knowledge. We played Authors, Flags, and other games where there were right answers; we listened on the radio to the "Quiz Kids" and "Information Please," competing with child and adult contestants; we accumulated points at Sunday lunch, the one meal in the week we ate together, by flashing questions at each other. The message was: having brains and using them is of value.

At twelve I entered the Brearley School in New York City, where I was to stay for the next five years. It was an all-girls school. The argument for single sex schools for girls and young women is that, freed from the need to please boys, not needing to hide everything having to do with prowess and competitiveness in "male" areas, girls are able to excel in leadership, sports, science, and whatever else they wish to attempt. My experience at Brearley makes me believe that is the case. Yet most of my classmates worked briefly after college graduation, then married and withdrew from the working world. Such schools may have equipped young women for competitive professions, but most of my classmates did not pursue such careers. So how does this help answer my question about how and why I did?

At the Brearley our teachers were competent, often inspired, in their subject areas. But few were married; they were mostly maiden ladies. Richard Howard has described some of the women teachers of that period as sibyls. One is in awe of sibyls, may learn a great deal from them. But I didn't want to be like them. Emily Dickinson, the only woman poet before my own time whose work I loved and still love, became identified with them: the spinster of Amherst with her mysterious spells. If only I could have the sense of the unexpected in my poems that she had in hers, and the miraculous condensation, and. . . but I didn't want to be like her.

I did want to be like Mrs. McIntosh, Millicent Carey McIntosh, the headmistress, married to a pediatrician, mother of five in a family where everyone played an instrument, where they made music together. Perhaps most of us, at some time in childhood, wonder what it would have been like to have been born into another family. At six, I wanted to be part of the farm family pictured and described in my *Farmer in the Dell* book. It had an emerald green cover and waving lines of yellow-gold across the front—amber waves of grain? The farm family was large, and on holidays there were always plenty of brothers and sisters, aunts and uncles with their children, and grandparents sitting down at a long table, sharing a feast. In between, the family all had their assigned chores. As I was coloring the pictures in the book, I knew I envied that big, happy family. I didn't realize that I also wanted to be part of a world where each person, down to the toddlers helping Mother search for eggs, had important work to do.

When I was sixteen, Mrs. McIntosh's family became the one I wished to join. She was not only the headmistress who had rescued me from disgrace and punishment in my early days in an unfamiliar and rigid school, she was also my tenth grade English teacher. I loved her teaching—Chaucer, Thomas More's *Utopia*, Shakespeare—and she was my dream mother, presiding over my dream family.

That year, I offered to be her children's summer babysitter. As one of the school's misfits—overweight, rebellious, and Jewish—I must have seemed an odd candidate. Mrs. McIntosh told me gently that she never used students from the Brearley; it would be too complicated. Soon after I graduated, she went on to become president of Barnard. When I heard Jill Ker Conway I thought of Mrs. McIntosh, who must have been about Ker Conway's age—late forties—when I knew her. Neither of them was at all girlish, as many women in their forties (and beyond) still are. Brilliance and *womanliness*—the word seems too subdued, but I can't find a more appropriate one—shone out of them. And competence.

By the time I was in Mrs. McIntosh's class I knew that I would indeed go to Bennington. And that I would work. I thought that work would be singing. And for a long while it was, even though I enjoyed writing, particularly writing poems, and from time to time I would write. I have not fully answered the question as to *why* I moved toward work with such certainty. I don't fully know; such a question has no simple answers. But, having gone as far as I can with it, I'll move on to the central question, the "tradition" question.

When I speak of "tradition" in Eliot's sense—we must absorb the poetry that has preceded us before we can "make it new"—I imagine an image, a road paved with poems by men. An occasional path branches off the main road, poems by women.

Or instead of a road, a firmament of poets. Such a firmament was designed and published about twenty years ago (I think by *New York Quarterly*). In its center, tightly clustered, were the brightest stars, so indicated not only by position but by the large typeface in which their names were printed. As distance from the center increased, type-size diminished. I didn't disagree with most of the editorial judgments about who should be where, though they were, of course, both in importance and in number, primarily men.

So where do women find their tradition? One could say they find it on the main road or in the center of the firmament, and that they are fortunate to be both a part of that tradition and separate from it. To understand why I say they might be fortunate, it might be useful to look at one of the psychoanyalytic models for the tasks boys and girls have in growing up. Both genders (assuming traditional parenting) begin with the mother as the central figure in their lives. For those who will become heterosexual adults, the task for each gender is different. The boy must leave the shining object at the center of his life, the mother, but finds in his female lover a similar figure. The girl must leave the warmth and gleam of the mother for someone markedly different, the male lover. Thus the boy has one primary figure in his life, repeated twice (or many times), but the girl has two, because she need not give up the mother entirely in order to transfer her love to the father, and then her lover. Though this is a simplified presentation of a complex process, I believe it is adequate as a paradigm for considering the gender tasks of men and women poets.

If we look at poet-parenting for women poets, they have had as the central parent men, those males writ large in the clusters of the firmament. So again they must deal with dual love-objects, the poems of the father and the poems by themselves, whereas men have, again, only one-gender love objects. Perhaps this means that women have, in the Harold Bloomsean sense, less anxiety of influence. They bring the necessary revision of the influence with them because they are different.

I know that very early in my writing of poetry, soon after the awful Starnbergersee lines, I had a sense that I was influenced primarily by Eliot and Auden, but very different from them. The poems I wrote at Bennington were not my central preoccupation, focused as I was on a singing career. But though I have no copies of those poems, I remember enough to say they were directly related to poems I went on to write many years later when I put aside singing for writing. Those early poems showed my fascination with the collision of different voices which I'd loved in Eliot, the pleasure in wit and formal structure which I'd found in Auden, the wish for narrative from E. A. Robinson and Frost, and the attempt to capture some of Yeats' music—good luck, good luck, good luck, Cynthia (or "Goonight Bill. Goonight Lou. Goonight May. Goonight. Ta Ta. . .") —but they did not sound like poems by men. Nor did they sound like Stanley Kunitz, with whom I studied for a few months and from whom I learned a lot.

Men *and* women need both a matriarchal and a patriarchal tradition. Those a generation younger than I have one more evenly balanced than mine. But not balanced enough. How my individual talent would have developed in a matriarchal poetic tradition is almost impossible to imagine. Though to attempt to do so is as pleasurable as imagining myself as part of the Farmer in the Dell's family once was. Or as it was to create my own Utopia, an assignment Mrs. McIntosh gave us after we had read Thomas More's.

I am in a utopian landscape, leaning against my mother who is reading me a poem she has written. As I lick honey off my fingers, the music of her voice and words becomes the perfect air surrounding us.

But my imaginings of a matriarchal lineage soon founder. One-breasted Amazons enter, pregnant maidens come out of the woods weaving sage and matzoh balls into wreaths, a pleasant granny speaks from the oval office as Colin Powell salutes, and I give up, happy to return to the safety of Browning's Venetian palazzo where, without a matriarchy, I will write poems inhabiting any figure I wish. Not Elizabeth Barrett's, more like Browning's and Richard Howard's, but using my own embroidery needles and codpieces.

And why not? For some reason fiction writers are free to inhabit whichever characters they choose. Jane Austen, George Eliot, Tolstoy, Hawthorne, Flaubert ("Mme. Bovary, c'est moi"); nobody believes they can't inhabit characters of the opposite sex. There does seem to be a different expectation for poets; they are seen as more tightly entwined personally with what is in the poem.

This is a subject for another essay—although it could connect to this one, because it makes me wonder why the life histories of women poets, such as Dickinson or Amy Lowell or Marianne Moore, were important to me from almost the beginning of the time I wrote poems, and the life history of Eliot, Auden, or Yeats carried little weight until very much later. Another question posed but unanswered.

Perhaps there is a hint of an answer in a paragraph in a *New York Times* article entitled "Hillary Clinton's Debut Dashes Doubt on Clout": "Mrs. Clinton's experiences in Arkansas and in the 1992 campaign have taught her she must try to avoid appearing elitist or like 'the yuppie wife from hell,' as a magazine put it. She has tried to offset her role as a policy maker by encouraging publicity about her attention to state dinners and her daughter's soccer games." So for a woman poet who wants to ignore society's expectations for her, perhaps the life of a male poet with whom she identifies is irrelevant and the life of a female poet, who might play the same role, must be scrutinized.

There is another aspect to the road paved with male poems, the firmament of male stars. To whom do we, women, address our poems? All poets write to speak to someone: first the self, but then another.

Here we get to the point Eavan Boland makes so touchingly in "The Woman Poet: Her Dilemma," when she describes the voices that interrupt a woman as she tries to write about a child and some laburnum pods. She feels torn between intensifying the romantic moment, thus undercutting that which is ordinary and routine (the pull of the male romantic tradition)— and inserting some anger into the scene (the pull toward a separatist feminism). The voices Boland hears urging her this way and that are internalized voices, the same ones that once told you to be a good girl, the ones who now may love and admire what you write or reject it. These voices urge women poets to be a certain way if they want to be loved and admired.

Boland's voices are rooted in a particular time in the twentieth century, a time akin to mine, though she is somewhat younger. The point is not whether they are accurate for everyone—but I believe them to be a part of the tradition that must be acknowledged, even if rejected, by poets born before World War II. Women (and men) born after that time hear an increasingly diverse choir of voices. Even so, many of the same problems with "the tradition" remain.

If women poets wish to be loved and admired, and I believe all do (men do, too, but what they must do to receive love and admiration may be different), how does the wish affect what women do? Judging from the results—that is, the women who have been loved and admired by those in the center of the firmament—there are several categories which encourage that love: girl (no matter what age), spinster, or safely meek woman. Lesbians will, of course, have different love objects, but they, too, can be admired by those in the firmament if they are not fighters: Elizabeth Bishop and May Swenson rather than Muriel Rukeyser or Adrienne Rich. What category is missing from this list of acceptable women? Heterosexual women who wish to have what men have: full participation at the center of the firmament and who neither remain girls nor are safely-meek. Perhaps these women are seen by men as mothers, Bly's dreaded "tooth mother naked at last."

In addition to the owners of the voices Boland describes, there is another person for whom one writes, another person one wants to please, even to enchant This voice belongs to a real person or people, the "sympathetic Other—or others," who Maxine Kumin says "provide a balance point." This Other is one's ideal reader. All poets have them; even solitary Emily struggled desperately to find at least one. I am fortunate to have several. Richard Howard came first, followed shortly after by Jane Cooper, and more recently by Edward Hirsch. Both my children from time to time play the ideal reader role. Sometimes, usually briefly, a lover has. These ideal readers are counted on for criticism as well as praise. But the wish to please them is unequivocal. The wish is to make each poem something which they will receive with delight, responding: "What a poem!"

What one wants to see in the face of the ideal reader is what a toddler looks for in the face of the mother when she or he presents a mud pie, a piece of paper full of crayoned scrawls, or a teddy bear festooned with toilet paper. The toddler's face is alight as she lurches toward the recipient. Her eyes scan her mother's face. If the mother responds with pleasure, all is well. If not, the child is dejected. The light drains from her face. The offering may be abandoned or destroyed.

I have called the recipient of the toddler's gift "Mother," and the toddler "she." Does the ideal reader's gender matter? Perhaps, but I don't know how.

I go back to singing as I ponder how the recipient of an offering influences the making of it. Response to performance is so much more immediate than it is to a poem. (And gender doesn't matter: Susanna is a women; Figaro, a man; Cherubino. . . .) Performers often describe feeling waves of love flowing toward them.

When I was twelve I stood alone on the stage at the Brearley School and sang: "I wonder as I wander out under the sky/ Why Jesus our Savior has come for to die/ For poor lonely people like you and like I. . . ." It was my first year at the school and I did feel poor and lonely. The applause rang out when I finished; it seemed louder than the loudest Christmas bells. For many years after, people who had been at that concert would praise my singing in the most extraordinary terms. Yes, it felt like a kind of acceptance and love. But the singing of that song was not such a simple and direct way to receive what I had longed for.

One reason that I never felt I belonged at the Brearley was that I was Jewish, one of five or six Jews in a class of fifty. Was Jesus my savior? So now, I've come full circle: answers to complex questions risk oversimplification. And the seemingly simple questions elicited by pondering Eliot's "tradition" in relation to women turn out to have been explorations which have yielded tantalizing tidbits— good name for dry dog food—with definitive answers always just out of reach. In the end, I feel I had two choices as a poet, though this realization has been provoked—I choose the word advisedly— by writing this essay. The first choice can be exemplified by telling the story of the New York man, the Jewish tailor, and the suit.

A New York man goes to see a Jewish tailor (I'm not sure why either is so designated; perhaps in the tailor's case for the pleasure provided by the Yiddish accent, or perhaps anti-Semitism is embodied in the joke). The man wants a suit made. When he goes back to pick it up, he tries it on and finds one arm is much longer than the other, so long that his hand can barely be seen. Distressed, he points out to the tailor that one arm of the suit is much too long. The tailor reaches up the arm of the suit until he finds the man's hand, takes hold of it, and pulls down the previously hidden hand until it emerges. The man is now lopsided. The tailor convinces the customer that now everything is fine, but in a moment the man notices that the other hand has disappeared. The tailor tells him to assume a different position which remedies that difficulty but causes one pantleg to drag on the ground. The pattern of the joke continues, with the tailor pulling the man this way and that until he is a pretzel and can hardly walk. The man leaves the tailoring establishment to go to the subway. Two bystanders watch him. One says, "Look at that poor fellow—so deformed." "Yes," says the other, " but what a beautifully fitted suit."

The second choice I had, and I believe it's the one I took, was to say the world is a rich and marvelously varied place; I want to take as much as I can of what it has to give. I'm greedy. The world is my oyster; I want pearls and mother-of-pearl and rough shell and barnacles and, of course, the slimy, viscous inhabitant. I'm greedy. Where's the Tabasco sauce? I'm going to be a singer, I'm going to be a poet, and, most recently, I'm going to be a psychoanalyst. The world is mine; I'll find what I need when I need it.

And I think I have. Yes, there was Mosaic law, patriarchal law in both the last choices—poet and analyst. But if I loved Eliot, I loved him; if Freud's discoveries of the unconscious, free association, and transference seemed to me amazing and true, so be it. I took what I could from each and left the rest. I couldn't use Eliot's Anglicanism or Freud's vision of women as stunted men, and I didn't need to. I was free to pick up whatever I needed anywhere in the world. To say this is to risk grandiosity. I know it, but it is how I experience my life as maker., No capital M. Just the bits and pieces, gathered, arranged as best I can into mosaics.

ON RECLAIMING "THE UNIVERSAL"

Suzanne Matson

As a graduate student and teaching fellow, I shared a series of offices with other women. Whether the powers that assigned offices wanted to discourage affairs between graduate students, or, as we joked, make it easier for women teaching fellows to pull up their pantyhose between student conferences, I do not know, but the single-sex office pairings had the effect of encouraging lively exchanges about issues pertinent not only to our lives as graduate student teachers, but as women graduate student teachers. I see this more clearly in retrospect, because for a long time I resisted the idea that being a "woman" anything—teacher, writer, student— was one whit different from being the thing itself. I would not have considered that as women graduate students or teachers we had any issues that set us apart from our male peers. In the same vein, taking Elizabeth Bishop's stand, I felt that as an aspiring poet I surely would refuse to be in any "women's" anthology of poetry; I believed that making such a point of gender was demeaning to the literary work of women, and consigned their efforts to a secondary level.

My staunch support of "universal" values in literature stemmed from my accumulated education; certainly it received massive doses of reinforcement at key junctures. I showed my first undergraduate poems to a professor who did me the service of taking them seriously, commenting on them as if I had a potential vocation as a writer. He offered valuable advice about rhythms, line breaks, word choice, poetic clichés. Then he turned his attention from form to content, and the tone, as he proceeded to warn me about overdoing something, was confidential—almost man-to-"man." My reaction was swift and overwhelming: *of course* and *how stupid of me.* He talked about the importance of audience, how the writer should not narrow his range of address, but have before him the goal of being "universal." He was referring to a couple of poems in the stack that were about sexual violence. I think it was at that moment that I disavowed "women's writing"; at the same time I felt absurdly grateful for his frankness, which I was sure had saved me from an embarrassing trap. Vaguely, too, I was flattered: he had referred to me as if I had real readers—readers whom I would not want to alienate (bore, disgust, irritate) by writing only as a woman. This second level of his critique after craft had had to do with the very approach of the poems: the voice, the vision, and the inherently female quality of the experience. And yes, the anger, which he wished were taken out. In my rush to meet him more than halfway, I wished I had never put it in.

Interlude: The summer before graduate school I had enrolled in a poetry workshop taught by a Famous Woman Poet. I did and still do admire her work enormously. One day in class, she responded to a student poem in front of her by musing aloud, "Don't write too many kitchen poems." *Be universal,* I chimed in mentally.

In graduate school, my first literature courses focused on those four monuments of modernism: Pound, Eliot, Stevens, and Williams. Because each poet but Stevens came with his own epic, and every one of them had authored his own critical prose as a kind of concordance, they defined not only the poetry of Modernism for me, but the essence of *serious poetry* itself. Real poetry was massive, manifestoed, as layered as geological strata, free from "emotional slither," "impersonal," and driven by the imagination coursing like a "noble rider." Anti-heroes were the modern urban cousins of classical heroes, and one man could figure so large in a poem as to be confused with a town, a river, a whole landscape. I looked up Greek myths, Arthurian legends, and old political scandals—references that were to me remote and paper-thin. Dimly I heard the poets speaking to me from behind their masks.

These spokesmen of modernism had their differences, but they had defining areas of agreement: rejection of the subjective mode and the body, displacement of the "self" into masked speakers, a technical hygiene that preferred objective over discursive language structures, and identification with tradition at the same moment they were claiming to "make it new." H. D., a quintessential modernist herself from Pound's first naming of her (*H. D., Imagiste*), began her poetic career scrupulously aligned with principles of suppressing the self in the text. Later, as she worked herself out of Pound's direct line of influence, she wrote from a distinctly gendered and embodied—if masked—point of view. Still later, some of the classical masks came loose, and that is the work of hers to which I gravitate. This curve of H. D.'s career suggests to me that the aesthetic she had begun with was not her own, and that her struggle to find a way to bond with tradition enough to "make it new" was a double task that required her first to invent a female line of access to it. It seems significant to me that the only H. D. we read in seminar, as a footnote to early modernism, was the technically spare and concrete poet of "whirl up, sea"—the same poet who had gained Pound's imprimatur in 1912.

At the same time I was being introduced to the modernist canon in graduate school, I was developing my own reading lists from the poetry sections in bookstores: Elizabeth Bishop, Sylvia Plath, Anne Sexton, Adrienne Rich, Sharon Olds, Sandra McPherson, Jorie Graham, Louise Glück, Jane Shore. The list grew every day with new voices on the scene, excitingly close to my own age: Katha Pollitt, Sharon Bryan, Maria Flook, Heather McHugh, Olga Broumas, Laura Jensen. My women friends and I traded tips and lent each other books. *Have you seen this? Read this!* These poets mattered to me so much that I wanted to linger over every line— though I could not turn the pages fast enough—and their work invariably sent me back to my own writing desk, thoughts and adrenalin racing. I hungered for their next books as if for food. Clearly I had been starved for a type of lyricism that modernism disdained. The male poets I bought and read—Richard Hugo, Robert Lowell, C. K. Williams, William Matthews, Marvin Bell— were also poets whose voices emanated from a model of a grounded, coherent self. Yet I read the women poets more, and more fervently; simply put, they were the ones who made me want to write.

Why would this be so? The answer must lie in a woman poet's relation to tradition. There was, in these poems by women (about fathers, mothers, lovers, the body, sexual passion and sexual violence, a moral opposition to suffering, the difficulty of finding a voice, the resistance to inherited language, the power of fecundity and ambivalence toward it) a large permission to write from my genuine point of view, a specifically female one. These were not poets who had "solved" the problem of speaking to the tradition, but, excepting only Bishop, Plath, and Sexton, were daily going about the business of solving it. The task remained open, active, full of friction and energy.

Certainly the fact that I "studied" male poets and read—not exclusively, but to a large degree—female poets for my own poetic well-being had to do with both the handed-down world and these changing forces of the new. Eliot says, in "Tradition and the Individual Talent":

> No poet, no artist of any art, has his complete meaning alone. His significance, his appreciation is the appreciation of his relation to the dead poets and artists. You cannot value him alone; you must set him, for contrast and comparison, among the dead. I mean this as a principle of aesthetic, not merely historical, criticism. The necessity that he shall conform, that he shall cohere, is not one-sided; what happens when a new work of art is created is that something happens simultaneously to all the works of art which preceded it. The existing monuments form an ideal order among themselves, which is modified by the introduction of the new (the really new) work of art among them. (p. 38)

On the face of things, these words should lead us to feel optimistic. After all, as a male professor asked me once, if Adrienne Rich really is a great poet, does not Eliot's model provide for her place in the continually reshuffling "ideal order" of "monuments"? At the time, I agreed. But now I am not so sure that "tradition" in Eliot's sense is a model that satisfies me.

First of all, I would have to search below my casual automatic "translation" of the male pronoun—the poet and "his complete meaning." Surely we all *know* that "he" is neuter in this convention of written English, and that "he" is meant to be "universal." If *he=the universal*, does that mean, as it must, that the *universal=he?* What is implied by this learned reflex of the reading female? Is the *she* erased, or is she translated? If the former, then what happens to her? Where does she go? Does she disappear into the thin-air dashes and dark secretary drawers of Emily Dickinson? Did she exist in the first place? If *she* has been "translated" into a universal *he*, what has been lost in the translation? Does translation require disguise, a kind of cross-dressing into the apologetic self-mockery of Anne Bradstreet, or the scholarly impersonality of Marianne Moore?

My point is that Eliot's whole "ideal order" claims to rest upon his theory of the impersonal, that distillation of flesh and blood into the abstract artist. I do not know whether this sloughing off of the body, the personal, is possible—or even desirable. Certainly Eliot's own work seems gendered to me, as seen for example in *The Waste Land*'s heroic quest metaphors, or his poems' general preoccupation with beguiling-but-dangerous female figures. We can go beyond this to say that the fact that Eliot can incorporate the "monuments" of tradition so seamlessly into his own poetic voice indicates a lack of quarrel with those inherited male voices; rather, he perceives a match. As the modern poet, he will continue probing the Great Western philosophical and moral questions while also exploring the psychology and anthropology of the twentieth century. It is a tall order, but the poet has a team of players behind him, Virgil and Dante right at his side, and the assurance of *being* the universal pronoun. There is no energy wasted in fretting that the "tradition" was not in his language to begin with.

Eliot's own words allow for the possibility of "the really new" work of art disrupting the prevailing order, and I think that part of what is "really new" about Plath, Sexton, Rich, Olds, Glück, McPherson, and so many others, is the presence of the poetic voice speaking from the female body. This sense of a voice *grounded* in the female is what drew me with such force to these poets ten years earlier, and what finally persuaded me to abandon my self-deceiving notion of the "universal." Insofar as we can give voice to the universal, we can articulate human drives to satisfy hunger, procreate, shelter ourselves, and find ourselves in relation. But in exploring these conditions of the human, I have come to recognize very different approaches in myself and in other women poets from the prevailing "tradition." If it were simply a matter of filling in female experience—i. e., writing the great childbirth poem, retelling fairy tales from female points of view, talking from the wife's and daughter's seat—we could have all relaxed after Plath's "Three Women," Anne Sexton's *Transformations*, and Rich's "Snapshots of a Daughter-in-Law." Continuing to document experience from female points of view is of course vitally interesting and necessary. But it is not simply a matter of fill-in-the-blank, and then presto, move into your niche in Eliot's mega-story Tradition Towers.

Perhaps I do not wish to live in a tower. Which brings me to a story. When I was reading Continental fiction in an undergraduate tutorial, my professor, who had created my extensive reading list, asked me to rank some authors we had recently read in terms of greatness. It was not a trick question, and probably only half-serious, but for him, the process of ranking genius was a productive heuristic, generative of useful measures and definitions of value. The question put a freeze-frame on my thinking. The problem, if you could call it that, was that I liked everything we had read, for different reasons. Tolstoy, Turgenev, Dostoevsky, Balzac, Zola, Stendahl, Flaubert, Proust—who could choose? Who would want to? By way of answer I could only catalog my full flush of admiring responses to the works. He told me I had catholic tastes, and I had to go away and find a dictionary to discover that with a small *c* my appreciation was "comprehensive, universal." In making the remark there had been something in his friendly, paternal tone to suggest that intellectually I was not yet fully formed, and did not know my own mind. The irony that strikes me now is that apparently there were two "universals," one to be striven for, and one to be grown out of: the former had to do with the both-genders *he*; the latter with an attitude of sympathetic receptivity intellectually inferior to a muscular mental posture of agonistic struggle.

My younger self left that conversation feeling chastened, and resolving to develop a "critical consciousness." But I must consider now the possibility that Eliot's agonistic model of hierarchy and monumentality better fits the male imagination, along with Harold Bloom's Freudian metaphor of literary patricide. More natural to my own conception are Nancy Chodorow's psychological paradigm of an enduring daughterly bond to the maternal,[1] as well as Elaine Showalter's discussion of female tradition in terms of a "quilt," with its suggestions of extension, adjacency, and collaborative artistry.[2] But finally, each model is a frame we impose upon literary phenomena, multiplicity, and generation. Tradition cannot but mean all that we choose to remember. What matters fundamentally is acknowledging each vision, freeing vision from the distorting prescription spectacles of the male "universal," and letting *universal* take back its wholeness, its comprehension, without the hegemony of the defining "the."

NOTES

1. *Feminism and Psychoanalytic Theory* (New Haven: Yale U. Press, 1989), pp. 57-65.

2. *Sister's Choice: Tradition and Change in American Women's Writing* (Oxford: Oxford U. Press, 1991), pp. 174-75.

IF WE LOOK FOR THEM BY MOONLIGHT

Colleen J. McElroy

It is almost too simplistic to begin this essay with a line I've used so frequently in the past to describe my first contacts with poetry, but here goes: I was educated in a school system that led me to believe all writers were male, white, and dead,—three conditions I had no wish to assume. There. I've said it. What I consider tradition does not fall within that formula. Those literature courses I could endure presented poems as exacting, technical little snippets of obscurity and abstraction. Those courses neglected my world and the people in it, all the women in my family—my grandmother, my mother and her sisters—women who wove wonderful tales of truth and love, life and death. Yet it is because of those women that I have become a poet, or more precisely, a storyteller.

I grew up with women who were storytellers. They talked in parables and never answered a question with a simple "yes" or "no." All my mother needed was a key word to begin a quote from Shakespeare: Can I go out? What is that? Where are you going? Any of those brought forth passages from the bard as my mother answered: "Out, out brief candle," "What is this I see before me," "Where upon I take my leave. . . ." And her sisters, sitting around my grandmother's oak table almost every weekend, viewed all subjects as fair game for a story: the way rice was meant to be cooked, why so many flies hung around a certain neighbor's door, my grandfather's job at the Anheueser Brewery, a cousin's surprise pregnancy, or the secrets of Farrow, the neighborhood grocer. Their stories were full of secrets, at least where I was concerned. If she thought I was listening too intently, my mother would say, "The walls have ears," and the women would start talking in metaphors.

Under the guise of offering a recipe for some dish they knew I wouldn't like, they'd abandon old man Farrow in a sea of okra— "Slimy as all get out," they'd mutter. On other days, they'd condemn a wayward cousin to a lifetime of tripe and pigtails. "Some folks just cozy up to any old thing," one would say. "Un-hun, I hear that," another would answer.

Then they'd look for me, squatting under the table, its legs as brown and thick as theirs, a box of crayons and a coloring book in my lap as I pretended to be busy. I'd look up, big-eyed, feigning innocence, then go back to filling in the lines. Later, with my paperdolls, I'd imitate the entire conversation, complete with its nuances and cadences, intonations and inflections. In fact, when I couldn't remember the exact words, I relied on the rise and fall of syllables, making up words but letting the rhythms carry the meaning of all those adult secrets. With their sweet fondness for metaphor and storytelling, how could I not have become a poet?

Wait. All of that seems too clean, told as if there were a one-to-one connection between what went on in my grandmother's parlor and how I came to write poetry. Think again. There was still school to be reckoned with, and the women in my family believed in education—with a vengeance. They coached me in the manner in which they had been trained at Normal School—if there was anything normal about a system that set as its goals turning girls into proper young women who were "fit" for teaching. Along with my lessons on manners, I was taught to memorize, memorize, memorize. If those women had had their way, I would have memorized whole books. But I was a stubborn child, and to this day I resist memorizing anything. Was it the ritual, or the material? Perhaps it was simply being pulled away from my friends and into the house, my legs covered with scabs and the hem of my dress unravelling from spills I'd taken on my bike racing down the gravel path of the all-white cemetery. Yes, I knew I had a recitation in class the next day, but how could some old dead poet compete with the thrill of racing down Ash Hill? And how many times could anyone recite yet another tedious verse? I wanted excitement, like those stories I heard on the radio, with mystery and love, good guys and bad guys. Maybe that's why I took it upon myself to learn whole passages from Alfred Noyes' "The Highwayman":

The moon was a ghostly galleon tossed upon cloudy seas.
The road was a ribbon of moonlight over the purple moor,
And the highwayman came riding—
    Riding, riding,—
And the highwayman came riding, up to the old inn door.

"I want you to imagine England," the teacher said. "Imagine the gardens alive with spring blooms. The profusion of blossoms redolent with the smells of peonies and sweet william. Roses and lilacs. The full blush of calla lilies and violets. I want you to think of those English gardens, the country smells of hay and foxglove. Then I want you to imagine a poet walking past those gardens into the churchyard where tombstones stand in quiet repose. And imagine the poet's thoughts. What do you think he was thinking?"

Poet? Garden? Churchyard? Tombstones? The only graves I'd ever seen were in the cemetery at the end of the block. And we entered only when my friend, Bumpsy, dared the rest of us to slide down the gravel of Ash Hill and streak past the main gate in a hail of pebbles and out again before the gatekeeper yelled: "Get out! Get out! No coloreds. No Jews."

Maybe that white man in England was writing poems about how to keep colored folks out of his cemetery. That answer got me sent to the counselor's office, where I was told, once again, to remember the values of a good education.

In English classes, poetry and grammar were coupled like naughty children who had to be put in their proper place or else they might break the rules and run on, run loose, run wild. Sentences were tamed with diagrams, and any poem worth its salt could be scanned. I couldn't scan, but I could versify and signify, and on summer evenings when fireflies danced in and out of hedgerows, the boys waited to see how sassy the girls could be.

Once a year, we had Negro History Day. The world hadn't moved as far as Negro History Week or Month, and no one yet had thought to include our African roots in that celebration. We heard about Phillis Wheatley, and we memorized Paul Lawrence Dunbar and, when I was older, Langston Hughes. But when the holiday had passed, they were replaced by Coleridge and Wordsworth and Keats. Under Miss Crutcher's rule, we intoned every line without missing a beat. Miss Crutcher was tight-lipped and dyed her hair purple. Miss Crutcher believed in elocution. I swore she had a metronome buried inside her. How else could she recite all those poems—*tick tock, tick tock*—with idiot precision? Under her practice, I learned to hate iambic pentameter and all those forms that fixed words to the page so tightly, they seemed forever out of my reach. I swore off meter and rhyme and lines that hit on the measure. "When this class is over, I'm never gonna look at another poem," I said. But nothing is as easy as a promise.

> He whistled a tune to the window, and who should be
>   waiting there
> But the landlord's black-eyed daughter,
>   Bess, the landlord's daughter,
> Plaiting a dark red love knot into her long black hair.

My mother tells me I learned to read when I was three. She says she didn't know how well I could read until one day when we were on the trolley. In those days, preschool children could ride the trolleys for free, and my mother had announced when we climbed aboard, "My daughter's only three." The trolley was full, so we'd had to stand in the aisle. There were placards above the windows advertising all manner of things: Ipana toothpaste, Trushay (the before-hand lotion), Old Dutch Cleanser, Lux Radio Theater. I started at one end, reading just the big words because I was too nearsighted to see the others. But that wasn't the real problem. The real problem was that I read aloud, proud of my ability to pronounce every word correctly.

"That'll be a nickel," the driver told my mother. "If she's reading, she's paying."

I don't think I remember a time when I didn't know how to read. I read everything. I read voraciously and indiscriminately: Nancy Drew novels, romance and detective magazines, and comic books. After I was too old to crawl under the dining room table when the women came to visit, they'd find me hiding somewhere in the house—"Nose in a book," as my mother would say. One day my Aunt Jennie found me, once again, huddled over a comic book, a pile of them at my side. She snatched the book from me. "Girl, what're you reading?" she asked. But even she had to admit I'd shown good taste. Most of the books were "classic" comics, with a few, like *Wonder Woman*, thrown in to satisfy my need to find a heroine who, if not dark-skinned, at least had dark hair.

"Go in the front room and read some of those good books I got in there," my aunt said. And so I discovered Boccaccio and Poe, Nathaniel Hawthorne and Zane Gray. Under the topsoil of literary language, those stories were every bit as daring as the talk I'd heard at my grandmother's. I rooted for heroines cast in the shadowy realms of those risqué tales. And I cried when, typically, they lost the battle. At least Wonder Woman had the powers of Hera.

Sprinkled among the novels were a few anthologies of poems—*Best Loved* and *Greatest* the titles declared—all of them resplendent with elegies and odes from the likes of Shelley, Keats, and Wordsworth. I tried imagining those poets walking through the black section of town, *thee*-ing and *thou*-ing their way past the rows of brownstones and whitewashed stoops, past Bumpsy and that gang of boys who hung around old man Farrow's grocery store and the cemetery, past the vacant lots and poolhalls, past Miss Crutcher and Charles Sumner High. But I couldn't imagine those men grabbing their poems and coming down to earth anywhere near that spot I called home. The step from page to real life seemed too great. So while my teachers threatened me with failure if I did not live up to my potential, and my family warned me to get a "good education, something you can fall back on," I looked for books that competed with the world I saw around me—or, at least, with the world depicted in Saturday movie matinees, where the good guys and bad guys were easily identified and women were swept off their feet in heart-stopping romances. Those were the kinds of adventures that made the bawdy *Tales of the Decameron* all the more exciting. Even after I found Phillis Wheatley, almost hidden among the leather-bound books way down at the end of the bookshelf, I was too engrossed in Alexander Dumas' *Three Musketeers* and Pushkin's poems to fight my way through the stilted language of Wheatley's plaintive verse. Still, it was the excitement, not racial identity, that drew me to those adventures. It would be years before I discovered that Dumas, like Pushkin, had African ancestors.

Weekends, my mother's sisters gathered at my grandmother's house to sort out the world according to the stories they held. They sat around the oak table, the one my grandfather had ferried upriver on a flatboat, and talked about women who had defied tradition. In English classes, what few women we read seemed, somehow, variations of the same woman. After all, how far was Dickinson in her cultivated seclusion from the fragile Wheatley, who in privileged slavery was bound in servitude to the same class system? And the Millay I was offered served up dainty prophecies like elegant cups of tea. Their poems were whispers among the loud voices of male poets.

And how could "The Highwayman" ever have been the favorite poem of a black girl growing up in St. Louis? What seems clear is that in those years I had been so hungry for images of dark women that I had settled for Bess, the landlord's daughter, death braided into her black hair. And why not? Most romantic stories I'd read, from magazines to classics, wove true love and death as if they marched hand in hand, like Romeo and Juliet, Frankie and Johnnie. Like Bessie Smith's blues. Or Billie Holiday's sweet melancholy.

Between high school and my graduate years in college, my world erupted in sit-ins and demonstrations staged by coalitions of Black Power, SNCC, and women's liberation. Even Miss Crutcher, who had had a poem for every holiday, could not have found suitable verse in the old texts for these turns of events. Where could I have placed Phillis Wheatley, with her genteel rebuke of General Washington? Somewhere during that time I put aside the voice of Miss Crutcher and searched for other, more assertive voices:

> Around midnight
> if you stop at a red light
> in the wet city traffic,
> watch for us against the moon.
> We are screaming,
> we are flying,
> laughing, and won't stop.[1]

By the time I stumbled on women poets other than Emily Dickinson and Phillis Wheatley, twenty years had passed since my aunt had chased me out of comic books and into the leather-bound volumes lining her living room shelves. By then, I had fallen in love with a poet, and had taken it upon myself to please him by finding a poem to add to the wedding vows we were writing. I searched the old volumes, the *Best Loved* and *The Greatest*, for suitable verse. I'd settle for no more dark-haired women for want of seeing some part of myself on the printed page. I wanted women who took no stuff, like the ones my family had chewed on while I was growing up. But weeks later, I would have settled for a line, or even a phrase that would have brought me closer to home. Finally, I came upon Georgia Douglass Johnson's "I Want to Die While You Love Me." It was the first time I'd read a love poem written by a black woman. Something, I thought, something for me. A black woman who wrote about matters close to the heart. A sister whose language sang with all the elegance of any poet I'd ever read. A sister who saw herself in love and on fire with the joy of it all. But die? I swear I heard my grandmother's daughters sucking their teeth over yet another woman who had fallen victim to her own heart.

It is said that each morning Anne Spencer rose at the same hour, brushed her hair the exact same number of strokes, had her breakfast—with tea, of course—and retired to her garden of roses, lilies, nasturtiums, peonies, and marigolds.[2] There, she held time in check. There she considered the cruelty of the real world while she walked among the beautiful blooms rising out of rich black soil. The garden's enchantment did not mask the outside world, but rather brought the world's jagged edges into focus, sometimes mimicking the idealism of male poets, like Tennyson, but more often, maintaining those postures of etiquette that were proper for a lady—"Nice as a right glove fits," Spencer wrote. For once, I could imagine the poet walking among the profusion of flowers. Would I have been drawn closer to poems in Miss Crutcher's class had I known that poets like Anne Spencer grew their verse out of such familiar soil?

In the sixties I moved from the midwest to the west coast, from a landscape flat as an ironing board to mountainous country where fog hovered at the treeline like lace curtains, and the smell of the ocean engulfed the room where I sat, facing the window and an endless sky, while my poet husband read poems aloud. Romantic? Yes, but the poems were no romantic contemplations of nature, no poets on sublime walks through gardens. The language of these poems was direct, jazzy, and sometimes brutal, a world where beauty was as delicate and dangerous as walking a tightrope without a net. At first, the idea of a poet who still breathed the air of this planet was as unimaginable as the notion that I too would begin to write poems. At first I feigned interest, more entranced by the sound of my husband's voice, by the music of language, than by the poems themselves. Though I did not know it, my attention to the music and language was a first step toward becoming a poet. I was much more aware of the second step.

At least twice a month I attended poetry readings, some no more than coffee-shop gatherings of students and artists, some an overflow crowd paying homage to a celebrated poet passing through town on a a reading tour. Caught up in the excitement of seeing poets whose publicity, like that of movie stars, preceded their appearance, I joined the groups of habitués for intense discussion over cups of coffee, and reviews of anthologies with titles like *Making It New* and *New Naked Poets*.

Indeed, everything seemed new, but for me something was wrong, and one evening as I listened to yet another white poet claim to be speaking for all people—"white, black, green, or in between" is the phrase I remember—I realized I had not moved very far from most of the poets I'd read in Miss Crutcher's class. Despite the down-to-earth language, the black people who occupied the poems—from Negro gardeners and cooks to black boys running in gangs or hunted by angry mobs—were included with the same degree of significance as the scenery. They were cardboard figures with vaudeville dialects full of apostrophes to indicate missing sounds. They existed only for the immediacy of the poem and color of their skin, their inclusion no more than a cosmetic attempt to shift perspective from white to black. But where were the families? Where were the neighborhoods? Where were the heroes, the foolhardy explorers, the women like my grandmother's daughters? "Those are the stories I want to hear," I complained. And my complaints grew so strident, I was told to either shut up or write.

Perhaps I am fortunate. Aside from Miss Crutcher, I have had no classroom teachers to indoctrinate me into the art of poetry. My habits and traditions, good or bad, are those I've pulled off the path of self-discovery rather than the result of years of male-centered training. True, the poets I studied in college were almost always white, and most often male, their poems as predictable as a three-piece suit. And true, some black poets rightfully claimed their place in this enclave, pushing against their white counterparts by turning the language of white poets to the advantage of the black experience, as Sterling Brown did in transforming Carl Sandburg's line: "The young men keep coming on" into "Strong men keep a'comin' on/ The strong men git stronger."[3] But even while Carl Van Vechten sang Countee Cullen's praises, and Winston Churchill quoted Claude McKay in a speech rallying Britain to war— "Pressed against the wall, dying, but fighting back!"[4]—the works of Cullen and McKay never received the attention in this country that their writing warranted. Historically, black male poets have been set aside as examples of racial differences, lauded for their use of dialect or polysyllabic rhythms, but ignored in discussions of verse that was destined for the white male canon.

Black women writers have fared even worse. Like all women, they have been subsumed under the heading: Mankind. Furthermore, they are expected to confine themselves within a referential sphere where the black woman is depicted as mammy—namely, home and children—or whore—the hipswinging, fast-talking, sassy heifer. The more "universal" subjects of politics, culture, and religion are reserved for men. Thus, genderless, women shoulder the added weight of racism, "de mules of de world," as Zora Neale Hurston has written. It is a wonder that black women writers have continued to work at all under this double yoke, some plodding forward like Wheatley, some taking the bit in their teeth and shaking off that yoke as they walk toward a collective consciousness. None of this is without reciprocity, for just as Wheatley has been dismissed for not speaking in the voice of her people, writers like Sonia Sanchez have been criticized for having a voice too close to that of her people (and thus, not seriously literary). At a recent conference on African-American expatriates and Europe, the major premise of a male scholar's paper on Rita Dove was her so-called literary schizophrenia, brought about, he said, by her insistence on using "standard English" in poems about family and racial identity—as if language and the use of poetic forms were genetically determined. This same charge of literary schizophrenia has been leveled against such writers as Anne Spencer, Angelina Grimké, and Margaret Walker. Get back in that kitchen, girl.

Once, at a reading in Portland, Oregon, when I was one of the two women slated to appear, several well-known black male poets held forth during a dinner party prior to the reading. If the women offered a comment, the men waited until they had finished, then resumed the conversation as if there had not been an interruption. We were not asked to bring in the coffee, proudly served by the host, who pointed out how well he had taken over a woman's role, but we were not expected to contribute to the discussion either. After the reading, we were told our poems were "interesting." No further explanation seemed necessary. I still say that word with the bitter aftertaste of rudeness and burnt coffee.

> We need you—my Limousine-Lady,
> The bull-necked man, and I.
> Seeing you here brave and water-clean,
> Leaven for the heavy ones of earth,
> I am swift to feel that what makes
> The plodder glad is good; and
> Whatever is good is God.
> The wonder is that you are here. . . .[5]

When I began writing in the sixties, I genuinely believed I had set out on a lonely road. I was writing poems, but I did not fit the fraternity of poets present at readings I had attended. Even when the reader was a woman, she was not a woman of color, and no matter how passionately she attempted to speak of slavery or the drudgery of day work, it was from the privileged position of an observer. For want of living examples, I turned to the library to find poems written by black women. I believe I devoured every anthology of *Negro Poetry* I could find, and as soon as the anthologies of *Black Poets* began to appear, I devoured them as well. The works of Anne Spencer, Alice Dunbar Nelson, Gwendolyn Brooks, and a host of others began to nourish me. And when I read poems by young black women in newly published anthologies, it was as if I had uncovered some extraordinary *rarae aves*. Those poems seemed to leap from the page and take flight in words that spoke directly to me. I wanted to celebrate. I wanted those women to take me away and teach me their language, words that were *brave and water clean*. I wanted to shout: *The wonder is that you are here!* But I was too busy. There was too much to read, too much catching up to do after years of elevated verse filled with the concerns of Mankind, or poems in which pale women were drawn as some "quivering female thing."[6]

Now I began to discover more and more women poets: Anne Sexton, Muriel Rukeyser, Erica Jong, Denise Levertov, May Sarton. And, wonder of wonders, they wrote about taboo and female subjects: Sexton's "Ballad of the Lonely Masturbator," Millay's "Menses," Kizer's "Pro Femina." In the course of these discoveries, I also began to uncover African American women who seemed to step out of my past, as in: Gwendolyn Brooks' "Bronzeville Woman in a Red Hat," Lucille Clifton's "To My Last Period," Mari Evans' "A Good Assassination Should Be Quiet," Nikki Giovanni's "Nikki Rose." Had I come home at last?

I grew up in a world where images of African Americans were fraught with stereotypes. I began writing, late in life, because I wanted to break through those stereotypes, to show how varied and complicated the black experiences (yes, plural) are in this country, on this continent, on this planet. Over the years, I have learned to understand what was said between words, with body language and inflection, and most of all, with the music of language. Sometimes, when I labor over the rhythms of a poem, I still see Miss Crutcher, her brown face crowned in a halo of pale purple hair.

Lately, I have taken to reading mostly women writers. I do not avoid male writers. How could I? Indeed, why should I? We have a shared history. When Melvin Tolson evokes the images of "Hideho Heights. . ./ Frog Legs Lux. . .", and "A willow of a woman,/ bronze as knife money. . .," I truly believe his poem becomes, as he says, ". . . dangerous to/ the Great White World."[8] I know the urban chaos found in Ishmael Reed's poems, and when Al Young baits the reader with the up-in-your-face philosophy of O. O. Gaboogah, I am once again reminded of the biting sarcasm rising out of the stories my aunts told about the white women they worked for. Those stories armed me with a sense of language that I could not have gleaned solely from books.

I don't remember how old I was when I saw Marlene Dietrich in *The Blue Angel*, but it was the year the film was released, and I do remember sitting in a segregated theater, time and the bigotry of the outside world held in check while I watched Dietrich stroll across the screen in a man's suit, her fedora pulled low over one eye. The scene left me breathless. There was a woman breaking the rules, and I sat there in the dark imagining my own rebellion, right down to snitching my grandfather's fedora from the top shelf of the chifferobe. Writing has much the same effect on me, but whatever I do requires more than imitating someone else's style.

In writing, I hold time at arm's length and move into an imaginative world equipped with cadences and metaphors that are particular and peculiar to the life I know. But I am also aware of the temptation to imitate what I admire in others, or succumb to the conventions and expectations of some style that is deemed popular and acceptable. The trick for me is to stay true to my own style while I stroll through the mess of assumptions about how women write. Breaking the barriers of the canon is more than tailoring a man's perspective for female views. More importantly, as a black woman writer, I must resist attempts to define the writings of African American women only from the perspective of white women writers. The black writers who help shape my sense of tradition are not always found in the literary canon, but they are everywhere. As Ntozake Shange says in *For Colored Girls Who Have Considered Suicide When the Rainbow Is Enuf*, they are outside Chicago, Detroit, Houston, Baltimore, San Francisco, Manhattan, and St. Louis. St. Louis, my hometown, where my writing began, not formally but spurred by echoes of stories I heard when I was young.

When I write about the women in my family, I am all too aware of the world that waited for them when they left the safety of my grandmother's house. How could I not be? As a black child growing up during wartime segregation, a daughter in a family hungry for sons, I knew my world was held together by women. I may not have found black writers and African American experiences in the books I read then, but I had my mother's sisters, my cousins and neighbors, an extended family of storytellers: shouldering, blaming, shining, falling, fiesty, and good—and all of them feeding me tales full of identifiable heroes. That is also my tradition.

There are many of us now, black women bound to the sisterhood of poetry. The work of these women renews my insight and beckons me to share their sense of place and purpose. Our literary history, despite censorship and lack of recognition by those who espouse a canon, is strong and deeply rooted. But laying claim to a literary sisterhood is not an easy task. We must fight against both racist and sexist assumptions. We must cultivate our gardens, as Anne Spencer and Alice Walker urge, and we must also preserve our histories, oral and written, as Margaret Walker and Rita Dove have shown us. And like our sisters of spirit—Joy Harjo, Wendy Rose, Nellie Wong—we must recall our ancestors. Our poems must stride across the page, like Lucille Clifton's and Maya Angelou's, proud of their womanness, aiming to be warriors in the manner of Sonia Sanchez, Ntozake Shange, Audre Lorde, and Jayne Cortez. And if I have not mentioned some of my other literary sisters, it is not because I have fallen, once again, under the spell of canonmakers. I know you are there, rising on ribbons of moonlight, laughing, water-clean and strong.

NOTES

1. Jean Tepperman, "Witch," *No More Masks*, ed. Florence Howe and Eileen Bass (New York: Doubleday/Anchor, 1973), p. 333. Quoted with permission of the publisher.

2. J. Lee Greene, ed., *Time's Unfading Garden: The Life and Work of Anne Spencer* (Baton Rouge: LSU Press, 1977), p. 47.

3. Sterling A. Brown, "Strong Men," *Negro Caravan*, ed. Sterling A. Brown (New York: New York Times, 1973), pp. 390-91.

4. Claude McKay, "If We Must Die," *American Negro Poetry*, ed. Arna Bontemps (New York: Farrar, Straus and Giroux, 1960), p. 31.

5. *Time's Unfading Garden*, p. 176. Quoted with permission of the publisher.

6. Ibid.

7. Melvin Tolson, "MU" *Harlem Gallery* (New York: Harcourt Brace, 1922), p. 233.

PARENTAGE AND GOOD LUCK

Lisel Mueller

I was born in Germany, the older of two daughters of emancipated, urban parents who were wholly and blessedly gender-blind. My father always claimed that he fell in love with my mother when she slammed her fist on the table to emphasize her disagreement with a point he made. My mother was "feminine" in the sense that she was warm, outgoing and impulsive, but she was totally ignorant of "feminine wiles," such as manipulation of, and deference to, men. She did not use cosmetics and worried little about her appearance. I'm sure I internalized my parents' attitudes, especially since there was nothing about their friends to make me think they were unusual. Nor do I remember that in those families boys and girls were treated differently. What was perhaps important for my self-confidence as a girl also is the fact that we had separate public school education for girls and boys. I did not sit in a classroom with boys until I came to the United States at the age of fifteen.

And it was only after our arrival here that I was given to understand by American ladies that little girls and young women were supposed to be made of sugar and spice and everything nice. (We settled in Evansville, Indiana, which was quite Southern in flavor, and the time was the forties.) But by that time my behavior was set and I continued to live in obtuseness about the possibility of discrimination. Since I wasn't interested in becoming a lawyer or an athlete, I encountered no rejection. I did hope, when I entered college, to become a doctor and save humanity, but I did so miserably in my science courses that the plan was quickly abandoned. If I had been talented in that field, I'm sure I would have a long tale of discouragement and discrimination to tell. I switched to social sciences, in preparation for becoming a social worker, a field where women predominated—though that was far from my mind. It was my second-best chance to save humanity.

I was equally unthoughtful about the literary tradition. The past was the past—always unfair to women—but in my own college course in contemporary American poetry, taught by a woman, we used Untermeyer's 1942 anthology, which included a large number of women: Millay, Wylie, Moore, H. D., Teasdale, Amy Lowell, Louise Bogan, Leonie Adams, Genevieve Taggard, Muriel Rukeyser, Gertrude Stein, and others. And later, in the fifties, when I began to write seriously, there were many women being published. The majority of them are now forgotten, but so are most of the male poets who were prominent then. (Look at a list of Yale Younger Poets winners.) It did not occur to me that the tradition might exclude me on the basis of gender, and the fact that I was lucky enough to have my work accepted for publication quickly served to confirm that sense. Nor was I conscious of the fact that the editors and publishers of my work were—and with one exception, still are—men. If I had had a harder time getting published, that truth might have dawned on me.

I was, of course, annoyed by the patronizing attitude of men in general toward women writers during the fifties and sixties. One male "friend," who liked a witty poem of mine, expressed doubt that a woman writer could ever be *serious*. Another paid me his highest compliment by saying I didn't write like a woman. I was also aware of books by women, including my first, being subject to patronizing praise by male reviewers. Somehow none of this deterred or discouraged me; thick-skinned as I was, I thought it was just something that went with the territory. I did not believe then, any more than I do now, that we women stole the language; the language was always there, free for the taking, for any and all of us, women and men.

Now, of course, having lived through the Women's Movement and having taught young women poets, some of whom have remained close friends, I have become aware of the tremendous disparity in power, as far as the literary hierarchy is concerned, and the slighting of women in anthologies and literary criticism. Tokenism is often embarrassingly obvious: I have little hope that this state of affairs will change unless our whole society changes.

As a reader, I have gravitated more and more toward women poets. They give me pleasure: I can empathize with the voices. As a translator, I have been working exclusively with poetry and prose by women, partly for reasons of solidarity (they are, of course, underrepresented), and partly because of this empathy and greater depth of understanding, so crucial for trying to bring a writer's work over into another language.

REVISING THE FUTURE

Carol Muske

> Tradition is a matter of much wider significance. It cannot be
> inherited, and if you want it you must obtain it by great labour. It
> involves, in the first place, the historical sense, which we may call
> nearly indispensable to anyone who would continue to be a poet
> beyond his twenty-fifth year; and the historical sense involves a
> perception not only of the pastness of the past but of its presence;
> the historical sense compels a man to write not merely with his
> own generation in his bones, but with a feeling that the whole of
> the literature of Europe from Homer and within it the whole
> literature of his country has a simultaneous existence and com-
> poses a simultaneous order. This historical sense, which is a sense
> of the timeless as well as of the temporal together is what makes a
> writer traditional. And it is at the same time what makes a writer
> acutely conscious of his place in time, of his own contemporaneity.
> (p. 38)

I used to read this passage as if it were some sort of papal bull—
T. S. Eliot *ex cathedra*—allowing the uninitiated a glimpse of the
Covenant. Only lately has it occurred to me that what he's describing is something quite familiar. Familiar, that is, to poets who, after
all, truck in awe. He's delineating the poetic process: which requires that we step out of time, confront an essentially mysterious
universe, then recreate it in language. But why does this process,
mystical as it may be, have to carry the weight of generations
of literary precursors? That's a lot of people to crowd into one
inspiration: a little like those mindless fraternity gags, twenty
people in a telephone booth. And all that "historical sense," "generation in the bones" stuff: I doubt that Eliot himself really believed
that. We can say with certainty, reading his poems, that he felt the

power and timelessness of the poem, but the voice here is not that of Eliot the poet. This voice rather shamelessly dissembles: the rhetoric sounds judicious, but is emotional. This voice idealizes the initiate's "passage" into what seems to be a glamorous fiction of the New Criticism, an appeal for the depersonalization of art (which he likens later in the essay and rather too enthusiastically—in true Modernist style—to "the conditions of science") and his model for the simultaneous sublimation and aggrandizement of the poet's ego.

The first time I read "Tradition and the Individual Talent," as a young poet, I did not feel left out by Eliot's clear summons to the *man* who is poet, because I believed (à la Virginia Woolf) that the imagination was androgynous. Therefore, I assumed, Eliot *must* have meant to include *all* of us, male and female poets alike, in that one "man." And though I'd never experienced any such thing, maybe there *were* poets who felt Homer's breath on their necks as they lifted a pen?

Now I read these words and other, darker tones surface beneath the modulated official voice: for example, Eliot detaches himself from his own *drama* (this is after all a literary seance, a real table-rapper, dredging up the Old Guys); he offers us an oddly mechanical reduction of an ecstatic process, and then gets really *clinical*: he dequantifies Time, as in the popularized versions of Einstein's relativity theory. Linear time becomes spatial time or "timelessness" in time, as he puts it.

This historical sense (time *and* timelessness) provides Eliot's contemporary poet simultaneously with equality to and primacy over the past. The past is made manifest in the present, thus the historical is generative. Eliot says that tradition cannot be inherited, but the "labour" (!) which he insists is necessary to obtain it seems *given* and magical, like Arthur's freeing of Excalibur from the stone. The magic here involves conjuring the poet's "family tree" in a second: the literary equivalent of the selection process in genetics. What's avoided here is finally most present: the buried motif of birth, the birth of the poem. For what other metaphor, though hopelessly clichéd, still best represents the creative process, from inspiration (conception) through "delivery"? That Eliot stops short of it, that he will not name it, only serves to enhance its presence. One is tempted to conclude that in the absence of the

Other (code word for women), men are forced to give birth them-selves—to creation myths like this.

Harold Bloom offers advice here. He does not think that "sexual distaste or anxiety was at the root of Eliot's aversion to his own experience of poetic origins. Rather, he *dissimulated as all good poets seem to need to mystify in this area.*" (My emphasis.)

Well, yes. All good poets seem to need to mystify, those slippery tricksters. But this need seems to me to have less to do with protective camouflage and more to do with the poem's relation-ship to time. Eliot's concern with the past is familiar: he wants to set up a sanctioned order of succession. He is less concerned with the poem's natural affinity to a more inclusive *future*. But if it is possible to believe that every poem is a beginning, a moment of origin, then merely signalling the past into the present seems an incomplete gesture. As the poet H. D. said, in describing Freud's genius—he could make the "dead" live, but he could also *make the future live in the present*—thus releasing the pain of the analysand attached to either.

The future *in* poetry, or within an individual poem, is not necessarily connected to Poetry's own future. Every poet sitting down to write confronts the "blank space," paces on the cliff's edge. The future for us is inspiration, imagination—the silence before and after the narrative: what we move toward. Wordsworth spoke of the poet's need to look before and after him, and Shelley's poet-"seer" instructed politicians; Keats described negative capa-bility, the poet's ability to exist in uncertainty. Are we, now, still influenced by Modernism's iconoclastic sense of the past?   The modernist infatuation with classicism proved to be little more than an excuse for Hellenizing the fish-and-chips peddler and the so-called reclaiming of the common, the utilitarian, even the scientific, simply broke the future into fragments of contradiction. Despite the Futurists, the Vorticists, and Pound's cry to "make it new," there was no connection with what was to follow. In fact, there are those who would argue that Modernism destroyed the post-modern future in which we now live. Eliot said: ". . . the poet should know everything that has been accomplished in poetry. . . since its beginnings. . . in order to know what he is doing himself. He should be aware of all the metamorphoses of poetry that illus-trate the stratifications of history that cover savagery."[1]

And Eliot, when asked by Stephen Spender to describe the future, also foresaw this savagery *before* him: ". . . internecine fighting. . . people killing each other in the streets." From my present perspective in the city of Los Angeles, I find him most clairvoyant. But this bestial Tomorrow, as apprehended by Eliot, was not so different, for him, from what had come before. He was a man frightened of both father and son.

The female body has been appropriated for every kind of trope lately, and I desperately wish to avoid imposing yet another gender theory on it. Yet it's in our minds: woman, birth, and future, that the Other, the feminine, might provide a healing alternative here—and to resist this trope might seem to deny the source of our imagining. But resist it we must. It is just this kind of "temporary aesthetic manoeuvre," as Eavan Boland points out, that avoids the truth.[2] In fact, Eliot himself, in *Criterion*, referred to the poem as a "dark embryo." Extending the prenatal conceit, he said he was most concerned with making the past live in the *present* in a "reintegrated" manner. And finally, when all is said and done, he is less concerned with the integration of the past; he says it is the *present* that affords the most possibility of literary bonding: ". . . writers who are not merely connected by a tradition in time, but who are related so as to be in the light of *eternity contemporaneous*. . . . "[3]

"Eternity contemporaneous" sounds like a Catholic prep school, and in a way it was. Eliot acquired this take on the present at Oxford, when he wrote a thesis on the "associationist" philosopher F. H. Bradley. Far more than from Imagism or Pound, Eliot derived his poetics from Bradley, including his notion of the objective correlative. One of Bradley's tenets was that Feeling everywhere is trying to "reintegrate" itself into larger and more complete "wholes." (Everybody's conscious mind confronted these floating fragments of Feeling, but it took a poet's sensibility to fuse them.) The poem, for Eliot, linked the savage and the civilized; what psychoanalysis tried to do for the individual consciousness, literature could accomplish for the collective mind.

Eliot's obsession with the eternal contemporaneous begs the question about facing what is to come. (It is indeed a temporary aesthetic maneuveur.) The past is always depicted as *arriving*, ongoing—there is no tomorrow. With the past running in tandem with the present, we are doomed to repeat a history of fathers and sons ad infinitum, we are doomed to the stratifications of savagery and civilization, the endlessly mirrored self. Again, the temptation is to say that only by *getting past* the past—in effect, giving birth to another—can we redefine our relationship to poetry. I was tempted, in an earlier essay, to make such a claim.

In 1979, I reviewed Adrienne Rich's *The Dream of a Common Language* for *Parnassus* magazine, in a piece called "Backward into the Future." In my review, I discussed Rich's countermanding of the "historical order" in poetry, which was "the habit of viewing each poem written in the language as 'heir presumptive' to the tradition." It struck me that the "matrilinear heritage" does not seem to proceed "hiearchically" but "horizontally," as underscored by Rich's image of women passing a seed hand to hand. I quoted Woolf: "Yet I am now and then haunted by some semi-mystic very profound life of a woman, which shall be told on one occasion; and time shall be utterly obliterated; future shall somehow blossom out of the past."

I felt that Woolf was speaking to all women, as well as to her "spark" of *Mrs. Dalloway*—I felt I was on to something:

> Regarding "tradition," perhaps the aversion of many American poets to what is called "political poetry" may be, in part, fear of an altered sense of time's passage, fear, in particular, of a future. Certainly the desire to locate and define the past which obsesses contemporary poetry does seem predominantly male. The themes of the search for the lost father, the death of the father (heralded in the Oedipal criticism of Harold Bloom), the son's rite of passage and nostalgia for the nuclear family are all cloaked in ready-to-wear pathos.
>
> That is why Rich has asked us to "honor the risk" of her dream exploration out of time—accompanying that expedition requires us to move out of male history and tradition.[4]

The rather bald claims of this earlier essay, if reductionist, are sincere. The notion of time, and women writers freeing themselves from its contraints, seems as central to me now as it did then. It is important to know the past and the women writers of the past, but not with the sense of "civilizing savagery" that Eliot's tradition imposes. It is important to know these poets in the context of a *future* entirely outside history and its expectations. All poets believe in the timelessness of their art; it is women who are required to face this flow without a literary trust fund. It is precisely because of noninheritance—because we seem to be bastards, paupers, black sheep—that we are, at the millennium (or at whatever moment—look at Dickinson!), so free to face possibilities.

In 1979, I was interested in confronting the difference, if there is one, between Eliot's Past, or Eternal Contemporaneous, and a different kind of future. Now I'm not. Now it seems to me that "living within" a great poem by a woman might provide the best "future." Eavan Boland has written a poem called "The Journey."[5] The poem begins with a woman's voice, a mother's voice—"chastising" the past in the poem. "There has never been," she says ". . . a poem to an antibiotic"; and, "somewhere a poet is wasting / his sweet uncluttered meters on the obvious/emblem instead of the real thing." Every day, she says, "language gets less/for the task and we are less with the language."

The speaker then falls asleep over her books and Sappho steps off the page the poet's been drowsing over. The dreaming poet is led by Sappho into the twilight world (where Virgil has led Dante in the *Aeneid*) where the souls of infants who have died untimely deaths from "cholera, typhus, croup, diphtheria" float "suckling darkness." The poet pleads with Sappho to allow her to write about these souls, asking to be their "witness." Sappho replies, "what you have seen is beyond speech/beyond song, only not beyond love."

Thus Boland collapses time, guided by a great poet, into and out of the temporal, following Eliot's dictum—but the poetry (the poem itself) that derives from this journey teaches a lesson we have never learned in history—or the history of poetry. "Remember it, you will remember it," says Sappho. Then she seems to acknowledge a kind of "tradition": "There are not many of us; you are dear/and stand beside me as my own daughter." But it is Sappho's final revelation that provides new instruction, sets aside the ideal of literary transmission as ego: "I have brought you here

so you will know forever—the silences in which are our beginnings,—in which we have an origin like water."

Silence? To learn silence? To understand that the experience of
suffering may be beyond speech or song? But only learnable
through love? That language may be "less" than the task of loving? (Elizabeth Bishop to Robert Lowell, on the occasion of his
appropriating his wife's letters for his own poems: "Art just isn't
worth that much.")

And Boland's stance here defies its own dictum about silence,
but with profoundly different effect than, say, the "still point of the
turning world." The poet does indeed bear witness to the infant
souls, as well as Sappho's commentary. We do stay "in speech," "in
song," "in language," the poem remains very much a poem (written in traditional formal style), but the solar system has shifted
within the poem and we have a different "sun"—we are asked to
learn silence, to listen to it, *prior* to language—not beyond love.

It is a temptation: the desire to start over clean, as women and
writers. A whole new aesthetic. But it doesn't work that way. We
do live in history, we have, all of us, served our apprenticeships—
studying male poets, male literary history. There is much beauty
and pain and truth in what we've learned, and there are damaging
lies. The future we reinvent is dependent on our reinterpretation of
what's preceded us. Boland's poem, though it begins in accusation
and sorrow, ends up powerfully refiguring a vision of the *Aeneid*,
ends up rewriting the lessons drawn from the epic past.

What I've written here are musings: outside of theory. That is to
say, they offer not a strategy of women's poetry, nor a new tradition, but my own "history" of the future which is still happening to
us: the poem itself.

NOTES

1. *Atheneum* (Oct. 17, 1919), p. 1036.

2. *American Poetry Review* (March/April 1990), pp. 32-38.

3. Stephen Spender, *The Thirties and After* (New York: Vintage, 1967), p. 202.

4. "Backwards into the Future," *Parnassus: Poetry in Review* (Spring/ Summer 1979), p. 81.

5. Eavan Boland, *Outside History* (New York: W. W. Norton & Co., 1990), pp. 93-96.

THE ROAD OF EXCESS: MY WILLIAM BLAKE

Alicia Ostriker

Who is my William Blake? Or to put the question differently, what is the relation between a woman poet and critic and her most significant male literary Other? This essay will be a brief history of my romance with Blake. I will try, in other words, to describe my personal relationship with the English poet who for many years was the source and confirmation of my own strong-est thoughts, passions, and convictions—and who remains in some ways my deepest influence even though he is now the poetic father figure from whom I have broken away in order to do the work of my maturity, which is a woman's work. Father figure? No, more like a husband or lover, who remains a friend and ally after our separation.

We were introduced by a college roommate, and I found him immediately attractive. He might have been a man on a motorcycle crashing through the plate glass of the dormitory lounge. Or, yet more appropriately, a figure in tie-dyes and bells flashing through the respectable halls of Eisenhower-era academe, in those fifties famous for passivity and conformity. Luckily I never had to study him in a course, or our romance might have been nipped in the bud.

What did I like? First of all, Blake had the reputation of being "mad." I liked that. He wrote as an outsider; I liked that because I was one myself. His white-hot intellectual energy excited me, along with his flashing wit and irony, his capacity for joy and delight. "Joy" is a word Blake uses over and over again, and it is clear throughout his work that he believes joy is the absolute human inheritance of which we have been dispossessed. It seemed to me that Blake understood childhood better than any other poet—or at any rate was able to convey the intensity with which a child lives its life, without a trace of false solemnity or sentimentality. I loved his insistence on freedom for himself and all of us, and his faith that to constrict human freedom in any way is to separate us from the life of eternity and infinity to which we properly belong: "For every thing that lives is holy. Life delights in life." I loved his capacity to say outrageous things with the utmost casualness. Some of Blake's one-liners became my own dearest beliefs: "Exuberance is beauty." "Sooner murder an infant in its cradle than nurse unacted desires." "If the doors of perception were cleansed, man would see everything as it is, infinite." "The road of excess leads to the palace of wisdom." I still believe all of this.

There was nothing of the gentlemanly or genteel about Blake, nothing of the respectable. Much later, I discovered that T. S. Eliot, noting these same unregenerate qualities in an essay on Blake, finds them "terrifying." To me, a daughter of the post-Depression Jewish working class, Blake's nineteenth-century working-class sympathies were perfect. I had grown up pacifist and lefty, listening to Woody Guthrie and Pete Seeger. Among the songs of the labor movement I learned from my parents were the antiwar "I didn't raise my boy to be a soldier," and an antichurch song with the rousing chorus my dad used to shout:

> There'll be pie in the sky
> In that glorious land way up so high
> Work and pray, live on hay
> You'll have pie in the sky when you die.
> (IT'S A LIE!)

Where Woody wittily sang, "Some people rob you with a gun, some with a fountain pen," Blake sang even more globally, "How the chimney sweeper's cry/ Every blackening church appals,/ And the hapless soldier's sigh/ Runs in blood down palace walls." I was ripe for Blake's acerbic social criticism.

It was also extremely important to me at age twenty that Blake was so sexy. This was one of the things that made him less boring than, for example, Wordsworth. And though he was less lusciously erotic than Keats, or Spenser, or Shakespeare, he did something nobody else did, to my knowledge. He directly represented and endorsed female sexuality:

> What is it men in women do require?
> The lineaments of Gratified Desire.
> What is it women do in men require?
> The lineaments of Gratified Desire.

Blake in his notebook called this epigram "The Question Answered," and I concurred. Here at last was a male writer who knew that the bliss of sex was supposed to be mutual, not a matter of conquerer and conquest. More on this later, however.

Last but not least, there was the power of Blake's poetic style, of which the force and compression, the patterns of sound and rhythm, materially embodied the vitality which it advocated. "For we are put on earth a little space/ That we may learn to bear the beams of love," he declares in *Songs of Innocence*. Almost monosyllabic, utterly simple, "space" metaphorically standing for "time" and at the same time bringing cosmic vastness and our intimate place in it into the poem, preparing as well for the sense of a space through which the cosmic love rushes at us—and then the alliteration of "bear the beams" implying how passionate that love is, how actually hard to tolerate, yet how desirable. In quite another mode, my snort of laughter at the couplet "If the Sun & Moon should doubt/ They'd immediately Go out" came from a delight with the unconventional orthography and capitalization—and how they influenced rhythm—inseparable from the bold unconventionality of the idea. Throughout Blake's lyric and satiric poetry I found myself ravished by these fusions of meaning and form.

In graduate school I wrote my dissertation on Blake's prosody, discovering in the process that Blake's esthetics were as radical as his mind. At every stage of his career, from the early lyrics which sound so much like nursery rhymes, to the long-line, pounding, monstrous extravagances of his late prophetic books, the poet was solving problems of poetic execution, inventing forms to fit his visions. The dissertation became my first book, *Vision and Verse in William Blake*; what I called his "expressive" poetics, wedded to experiment, became my ideal. At around the same time, I stopped writing the formal poetry I had always written and began composing in free verse, which was harder.

My first ten years of university teaching, 1965-75, covered more or less precisely the time that is now thought of as "the sixties." It was the time of civil rights struggles and the deaths of Martin Luther King and Robert Kennedy, of urban upheavals and the Vietnam War. Young men in my classes were being drafted, were coming home mentally destroyed, their hapless sighs running in blood down university walls. This was the period in which political activism and idealism crested among American young people, along with the sexual revolution, the use of hallucinogenic drugs, and rock and roll. These apparently disparate phenomena were connected in ways Blake would have understood very well. It was easy to teach Blake. His poems were allegories of the life we were actually living. It was no accident that, for example, The Doors took their name from Blake, that a Blakean vision had inspired the young Allen Ginsberg. It was proper that record jackets and book covers used Blakean designs, underground bookstores sold posters of his paintings, and poets who did antiwar readings were Blake aficionados. Of all poets, he was our guru.

In the middle seventies, after finishing an annotated edition of Blake's poems, I began reading contemporary women's poetry. In the course of writing *Stealing the Language* I read a dozen or so anthologies of women's poetry, as well as upward of two hundred volumes by individuals. My life and poetry inhaled Sylvia Plath, Adrienne Rich, Anne Sexton, H. D., Denise Levertov, Maxine Kumin, Margaret Atwood, Judy Grahn, Sharon Olds, June Jordan, Audre Lorde, Ntozake Shange, Lucille Clifton—and dozens of other women poets whose brilliance and courage have transformed me forever.

"If one woman told the truth about her life," says Muriel Rukeyser, "the world would split open." When I started reading women's poetry I found a radical collective voice and vision equivalent to Blake's—equivalently outrageous, critical of our mind-forged manacles, determined to explore and rethink everything, and inventing poetic forms to embody new visions. I also found, I thought, a feminist connection. Looking at Blake with my new feminist eyes, I saw as his most striking characteristic his hatred of what we were now calling patriarchy, with its glorification of "rational" male rule (for Blake, Father-God-Priest-King are all summed up in the tyrant Urizen, whose name means "your reason" and "horizon"), its repression of sex and sanctioning of war, its victimization of women, children, and the poor, and its exploitation of verbal and symbolic mystification ("our world will be overrun without these arts," says Urizen) to justify and disguise its power. Blake opposes hierarchies of authority and rule, dominance and submission, restriction and repression, and identifies them with the masculine principle in culture which imposes these things on us. Redemption, for Blake, involved the reunion of male and female into an androgynous wholeness.

But there were some problems. I was, as I said, teaching Blake in the middle seventies. Reluctantly led by my students, kicking and screaming all the way, I was finally forced to recognize that Blake had a profound misogynist streak. The female figures he idealizes are always maternal, nurturing, and receptive rather than active. Some are victims of male violence, and they never fight back. His androgynous ideal is a male being who contains a female element, but never the reverse. His fear of what he calls "female will" amounts nearly to pathology in his late poems, and the structure of his metaphors is polarized and dualistic everywhere—even though dualism and polarization are what he is attacking. That is to say: Blake was a self-divided and contradictory poet, with real and to me very painful limitations.

"If the doors of perception were cleansed, everything would appear to man as it is, infinite," he says. When I was a girl I thought that by "man" Blake meant me. He did not. In fact his own perceptions were fogged in a quite standard masculine fashion. Able to perceive Man as infinite, he was unable to see Woman as equivalently so. Able to defend Man's freedom, he was unable to defend Woman's. Able to see Man as creator, he could not see Woman as anything but Muse.

To these discoveries I responded first with incredulity, then with anger. I stopped teaching Blake, stopped reading him. In retrospect this reaction looks to me like a postadolescent sulk, or, even more absurd, like the response of a child who is furious at discovering that her parents are merely human, not perfect. For I had needed perfection. I had needed Blake to be the perfect female as well as male predecessor. In some sense I wanted him to *know* what a woman knows, to *have done* the work which can only be done by women. I wanted him to have already done my thinking and feeling for me—even to have done my writing for me.

I recovered slowly. Part of the recovery came about through writing an essay describing Blake's conflicted views of sexuality, and realizing that his conflicts do not solve, but do exemplify, the contradictions of our whole culture. In fact, I started realizing that all great artists probably embody inconsistencies, because they do not censor themselves into tidy correctness. Rather than being angry at Blake because he has not already done my woman's work for me, I see I must do it myself—and that insofar as I pursue my own road of excess I will be extending what he taught me. To paraphrase Emerson and the *Baghavad Gita*, when him I fly, he is my wings.

If I look back at my own poetry, asking what is Blakean about it, it strikes me that readers unaware of my long discipleship might not make the connection. My poetic forms, styles, tones of voice, and lexicon, are nothing like his. What we have in common are attitudes toward reality, attitudes toward tradition, and some key themes: love and sex, social critique, a desire to imagine a non–dualistic, nonpatriarchal, nonoppressive world, a faith (against evidence) in what Blake calls "Divine Humanity," a belief in the reality of joy, a horror at war. Like Blake, I believe that the body and body politic are images of one another. This is the hidden subtext of my book *The Mother/Child Papers*, begun in 1970 when my son was born a few days after United States forces invaded Cambodia. What Blake calls "the torments of love and jealousy" and treats from a male point of view, I treat from a female point of view in several moderately tormented poems in *A Woman Under the Surface* and *The Imaginary Lover*.

A few of my poems are, like Blake's, the result of visionary experiences—though they are mere eyeblinks compared with his lifetime of gazing at the infinite. Like Blake, I enjoy comedy and satire. In the last few years, my work has become increasingly engaged with the Bible—reading it from a woman's perspective, grappling with its gods and patriarchs, trying to discover what I love and hate in this Book, and in my Jewish heritage. But Blake was there before me, reading scripture from his own radical perspective, defiantly calling his prophecies the Bible of Hell. And at least one piece of my manuscript-in-progess, *The Nakedness of the Fathers*, is a direct steal. I offer an intimate picture of what Solomon and Sheba were doing behind closed doors during their famous meeting. Among other entertainments, they talk; while he is inspired to compose the *Song of Songs*, she recites—a female variation on Blake's Proverbs of Hell in *The Marriage of Heaven and Hell*— Sheba's Proverbs, a woman's wisdom.

Paradoxically, I suspect that I have become more indebted to Blake after defining myself as a woman poet than before. Blake was a writer without an internal censor. I would like to be one. As I learn with the help of other women writers to defy or deflect the censor in myself, I feel increasingly related to Blake. He continues to propel me along the road of excess even while ceasing to accompany me. When I write most freely, I feel myself continuing his project of freedom.

Let me conclude by giving an example of a poem drawn from a woman's experience and in a woman's voice, which Blake himself could not have written, but which would never have been written without him. Among Blake's basic themes is the struggle between Reason and Energy—repressive Reason and passionate Energy— which enacts itself within our individual selves on a small scale, and in human culture and history on a large scale. In *The Marriage of Heaven and Hell*, Blake argues that these contraries are both necessary to human life, and that what we call Good and Evil are simply the principles of Reason and Energy—Reason demanding obedience, Energy in rebellion against it. Blake of course thought that there was altogether too much obedience in the world, and wanted to see the unshackling of Energy. His prophetic poems present these principles as mythic beings. Urizen is the repressive tyrant within our superegos and our cultural institutions. His is the "thou shalt not" to which we all submit, the fear of sin and transgression, the belief that we and everyone else should be orderly, the horror of broken rules. In his designs, Blake always pictures Urizen as an old man with a beard, rather like Michelangelo's God the Father. On the other side, the figure of Orc, taken from a classic term for hell—and an anagram for cor, heart—appears in Blake's designs as a literally flaming youth. The attractive and muscular Orc represents Desire, Energy, or Passion within the self, Rebellion in the drama of history. According to Reason, Passion is always of course horrifyingly destructive. Blake's view, anticipating Freud's, is that repression is the poison that makes it so. The more human passion is denied and repressed, the more destructive it must ultimately become.

One of Blake's earliest poems illustrating the conflict of Reason and Passion is "The Poison Tree" in *Songs of Experience*. In the poem's opening stanza,

> I was angry with my friend:
> I told my wrath, my wrath did end.
> I was angry with my foe:
> I told it not, my wrath did grow.

By the end of the poem, the repressed anger has grown into a tree bearing poisoned fruit, which the speaker's enemy eats and dies:

> In the morning glad I see
> My foe outstretched beneath the tree.

For Blake, this is a male drama. Anger and repression are for him both masculine characteristics. None of his female figures is ever identified as "wrathful," and none is ever shown repressing her own feelings. When female figures in Blake are cruel—as they often are in the prophecies—it is somehow always their nature to be so. But during a painful period of my marriage I found myself writing this poem, which certainly represents female wrath:

The Exchange

> I am watching a woman swim beneath the surface
> Of the canal, her powerful body shimmering,
> Opalescent, her black hair wavering
> Like weeds. She does not need to breathe. She faces
>
> Upward, keeping abreast of our rented canoe.
> Sweet, thick, white, the blossoms of the locust trees
> Cast their fragrance. A redwing blackbird flies
> Across the sluggish water. My children paddle.
>
> If I dive down, if she climbs into the boat,
> Wet, wordless, she will strangle my children

And throw their limp bodies into the stream.
Skin dripping, she will take my car, drive home.

When my husband answers the doorbell and sees
This magnificent naked woman, bits of sunlight
Glittering on her pubic fur, her muscular
Arm will surround his neck, once for each insult

Endured. He will see the blackbird in her eye,
Her drying mouth incapable of speech,
And I, having exchanged with her, will swim
Away, in the cool water, out of reach.

"The Exchange" was written because I was in fact canoeing one warm Memorial Day with my children and some friends on the Raritan Canal near my home when I saw this mental movie on the screen of my inner mind, was horrified by it, and could not shake it. Nor in fact could I forget the appalling image after writing the poem, for the poem was not therapeutic but diagnostic. One cannot count on poems to heal one's ills, but they are very good at revealing them.

My definition of myself at the time of this poem was a common one for women. I was a good wife, a tender mother, a firm pacifist. I was also an aggrieved woman and a martyr. The problems in my marriage were (of course) the fault of my husband, for I myself was above all (of course) a kind, loving, generous person. What the poem showed me, quite stunningly, was that I did not know myself. Here was this seductive and attractive murderess who was plainly also me. The woman under the surface was my will, my desire, my potential power as a human being, metaphorically submerged by me (by the taboo against female assertiveness which I had internalized), ready to emerge and produce massive havoc precisely because she had been submerged and resented it.

Here was a female version of repressed wrath, repressed energy, a female Orc—amoral in essence, forced into destructiveness by my denial of her existence. The fantasy of revenge and escape in this poem is one many women share, and many men fear. But part of what horrified me was realizing that the solution was no solution, that the fantasy left me a split self: what I recognized as myself would be "out of reach" of human love as well as pain, and the liberated goddess would be "incapable of speech," all passion, no mind. What the poem ultimately let me understand was that I needed to accept the submerged woman of power as a portion of myself, integrate her somehow into my above-ground normal life, and surrender my image of myself as oppressed victim. Needless to say, such tasks require years of concentration to accomplish, for they are more easily defined than performed. The role of victim has, after all, its glorifications; we cling stubbornly to our picture of ourselves as purely good and righteous. Nor do I suppose Blake would have approved of my conclusion. He too likes the image of woman as victim. Although several of his prophetic poems depict the reintegration of fragmented males, he has no equivalent females. Yet it is Blake who provides the model of the divided self which can be made whole only by uniting its parts. While I depart from his recipe for getting there, I must be grateful to him for imagining the goal.

In *A Room of One's Own*, Virginia Woolf claimed that "it is useless to go to the great men writers for help, however one may go to them for pleasure." Many feminist poets and critics today are separatists, believing that the language and literature we have inherited are so intractably masculine that women must withdraw into a women's culture in order to create freely and truly. For me this can never be the path. Too many male artists have inspired me by their attempts to be as fully human as they could—I cannot surrender my love of them, even if they failed. Doesn't everybody fail? Don't I fail too? A hundred and fifty years after his death, if Blake is looking down from his cloud, he might or might not approve of me struggling along on my own road of excess, looking for my own palace of wisdom. He is still, for me, a courage-bringer.

DEGREE AND CIRCUMSTANCE

Pattiann Rogers

I.

I feel that my life as a woman, a woman writer, and a mother has been, to a large extent, what I've made it, and it's been very blessed by the time and the society in which I live. In this section of my essay, I want to consider the issue of women and the literary tradition in light of my own personal experiences as a mother and a writer.

I admit there have been periods in my life that have been hard. Someone expected life to be easy? I came from a relatively poor family and married a man from a family of modest means. I worked six years, before our first son was born, to put my husband through graduate school. I did this because I chose to. I wanted to have children. Children were a goal for me, never a side issue, and I wanted to stay home with them and raise them myself. I made that decision. My husband had to be able to provide for us. I wanted him to feel satisfied and challenged by the work he was going to have to do for the next forty years. I don't regret any of these decisions.

Of course, it was difficult to write when my children were babies, toddlers, preschoolers. I had to write in any fifteen-minute snatches of quiet I could find, and that produced a certain kind of poetry. But these circumstances lasted only for a few years, not my entire life or even a major portion of it.

And I chose to have my children. Any woman living in our country today is able to make a choice about having children. Preventing conception is not difficult, and if a woman doesn't want to be a mother, that's fine. But I chose to have my children, and I knew they deserved a mother devoted to them, a mother willing to give them all the time they needed. While they were growing up, if there was a conflict, writing came second.

My children are the very dearest things in my life. They've provided me with some of the most ringing and jubilant moments I've known. They continue to do so. If I could go back and were offered it, a bargain with Mephistopheles, I wouldn't trade a Nobel Prize in Literature for either one of them. What a ridiculous idea! I wouldn't trade the experience of living with them for Shakespeare's talent. I say that with all seriousness. I feel this deeply about the value of the experience.

If, through caring for my children, I lost writing time, I gained by the expansion of vision and insight and compassion my experiences with them gave me. I've never regarded my children as burdens or a hindrance to my writing, separate or alien from it. They are a boon to me. Even in those difficult, demanding years of their babyhood, there was an exhilaration, an energy, a delight, an affirmation present in our house that I haven't experienced since. The writing I was able to do in those years is suffused with the energy my children radiated. I'll always be grateful to them for sharing with me their driving curiosity and love of life, for letting me see the world anew through their eyes.

And what is writing, after all? Is it an activity above human love for other humans, above obligations we have to those nearest to us? Is this what some men and women writers are telling other women? You don't need to let your families get in the way of doing *truly* important things. What is more important than loving and nurturing a young child who is in your care? Those who doubt the degree of its importance need only think back again for a moment on their own childhoods, on the lasting effect the adults who cared for them have had on their lives.

When the act of writing becomes enamored of itself, puffed up and arrogant, existing for its own sake alone, it ceases to be sustaining, perceptive, or fine. Writing must serve the concerns of "love and honor and pity and compassion and sacrifice," as Faulkner put it. What can be the value of a literature that is created at the expense and neglect of others? Literature is a servant; it must serve, and when it ceases to perform this function, it ceases to be a source of sustenance for the culture and becomes a rattling husk.

I didn't have a room to myself to write in until two years ago, but I wasn't hungry, ill, and working in a cold garret like Nietszche. I don't have a publisher waiting for my work, but I'm not an invalid like Alexander Pope. I lost writing time to raise my children, but I've never been imprisoned like Ben Jonson or Thomas More. I haven't had a steady source of income guaranteed for life, but I don't suffer painful and recurrent bouts of illness like Darwin. I had a pleasant childhood, not one of deprivation and humiliation like Dickens.

Writing is hard work, and most writers, males included, have had to overcome difficulties in their lives in order to complete their work. Obstacles placed in the way of writers differ in circumstance and degree, but to imply that male writers, who have made our literary tradition, led easy lives conducive to writing simply because they were males is to deny the facts of literary history.

And yes, it's true, many women who might have been great writers had unfulfilled lives due to lack of control over child-bearing and lack of opportunities and fixed social ideas. But surely we can't forget, we mustn't forget the many men who lived and died also without the opportunity to become writers had they wished—the many, many young boys, *boys*, who were conscripted and died or were maimed in wars (a victimization women in our culture have never had to face), men wasted in coal mines, on fishing boats, in hard factory labor, farmers with broken health, poor craftsmen, most badly nourished, without the opportunity for education. People have suffered in the past, all people, men and women, locked into their social classes, without choices, burdened by religious superstitions, beset early in their lives by diseases. To single out women as having suffered in the past seems to me limited in vision at best and self-serving at worst.

My father's mother died of tuberculosis when he was two. He subsequently was raised by a stepmother who had seven children younger than he. He received only an eighth grade education and was out on his own at fourteen. He was brilliant and creative, but he had to support himself and our family by whatever employment he could make for himself, one job after another. He spent the last leisure days of his life trying to write about religion and philosophy, with no formal background in either. Neither my father nor his mother nor his stepmother were treated very fairly by life, by circumstances. But I never heard my father call himself a victim, and he did everything he was able to do to see that I received the best education and opportunities he could give me.

Those of us, men and women, who live now in relative comfort and safety, who have never truly feared hunger or cold, who have the means to maintain our health, who are fêted and entertained and pampered like no other generation, we are obligated to write and work for all those, men and women alike, who died without ever having had an opportunity to express themselves.

And I need to say, before I conclude this section of my essay, that at nearly every step of my writing career I've been helped by men—teachers and editors and fellow writers—some of whom I've never met, who asked nothing from me but the best writing I could produce. I've been helped by women also, and I've felt a special relationship with them.

And there have been some men in positions of editorial and critical power who have dismissed my work casually, without giving it an adequate reading, but so have some women. Each event of this kind must be considered as a particular act committed at a specific time by an individual person. I can't think of it in terms of groups of people. Surely everyone will agree that when injustices occur, they must be discussed in a way that avoids condemning or demeaning whole groups of people or the accomplishments and sacrifices of individuals within any group.

II.

Now I want to point out an omission in our literary tradition that needs to be filled, and which I think can be filled. This is the serious lack of good literature written by mothers about mothering.

Of the women writers included in our literary history prior to 1950, the vast majority were not mothers. The Brontë sisters, Jane Austen, Dorothy Wordsworth, George Eliot, Emily Dickinson, Amy Lowell, Isäk Dinesen, Gertrude Stein, Willa Cather, Louisa May Alcott, Virginia Woolf, Edith Wharton, Edna St. Vincent Millay, Elinor Wiley, Edith Sitwell, Katherine Anne Porter, Katherine Mansfield, Dorothy Parker, Lillian Hellman, Elizabeth Bishop, Marianne Moore, Flannery O'Connor, May Sarton, Carson

McCullers, Eudora Welty—none were mothers, and of the few mothers who have written, (Kate Chopin, for instance), child-rearing is often denigrated or peripheral in their most noted works. I don't mean to diminish the value of the literature written by any of these women, but only to point out what is missing in our tradition as far as women's work is concerned, in order that we may have some idea of how to correct that omission.

One of the few major literary works by a woman and a mother that I'm aware of, that gives a fully-rounded treatment of the mothering experience, is the Kristin Lavransdatter trilogy written by Sigrid Undset, a Nobel prize–winning Norwegian novelist who wrote during the early part of the twentieth century. This trilogy follows the life of Kristin Lavransdatter, a woman living in the fourteenth century, from her childhood through courtship, marriage, the conception and births of her children and into their adult lives. The work is promoted as a historical novel, which it is. Although the translation I read seemed cumbersome and archaic, still there are spectacular passages of insight and vision in this work.

But what a loss not to have included in our literary tradition a wide and varied and thorough treatment of mothering, as well as other subjects, written by mothers. The nurturing of children—both physical and spiritual nurturing—is an activity crucial to the well-being of our culture, and it's an activity that engenders some of the most intense and enduring emotions ever felt by human beings.

Barbara Kingsolver, in an interview published in *Elliott Bay Booknotes*, describes these emotions this way:

> This person [Kingsolver's daughter] came into my life, for whom I would do anything, including throw myself in front of a truck, to save. What do I do with this? I have no idea, and I've been trying to figure it out ever since. I haven't stopped being a writer, in fact I've been a writer at the same time. I think my relationship with my daughter has given a depth to myself and, I hope, to my writing that I never could have hoped to have managed before. I never knew what it was like to love another person that much more than myself.[1]

There are few fine, serious and complete, artistic accounts in our literary tradition of the experience of mothering rendered by those actually involved in carrying out the endeavor. A comparable situation might be if half of the population were farmers and practically no one with experience of farming ever wrote about it.

I don't know all of the reasons why we have so few works of literature by mothers in our tradition. But before the middle of the twentieth century, to be a mother, for most women, was a totally consuming job, one that left little physical or emotional energy for writing; and, without reliable birth control, the bearing of children went on for years.

Also, for many women, raising children is a completely fulfilling endeavor. There have been periods in my own life when the accomplishments of my sons, their identities as individuals, especially in their adolescence, were so engaging and pleasing and satisfying to me that I was content in my life simply to help and support them. I felt no continual, driving ambition for work apart from them. I assume this can be true for other mothers as well.

But the fact remains that for mothers writing today, there is no strong and dominating literary tradition to support or guide the work. In addition, to write of the subject well requires overcoming the many examples of poor literature written on the subject, the woman's magazine and greeting card mentality. To write with power of the subject means creating new perspectives beyond the portrayals of mothers written by men, or by women who were not mothers themselves, that predominate in our tradition.

I find something in common with Marilynne Robinson, when she says, "I don't think I could have written *Housekeeping* if I hadn't had children. It was just part of my research."[2] My own children permeate my poetry, their influence most often disguised. But they are there. They taught me important things I hadn't previously realized about bodies, about maintaining life, about language, about how to delight.

One measure of the spiritual health of a society is the value it places on its children and the care it takes in protecting and nurturing them. When strong and numerous works by mothers enter the literary tradition, both the tradition and the society will undoubtedly be strengthened and enriched.

III.

There are times when a tradition can be more burden than mainstay. To bear the weight of established geniuses, to attempt to modify or abandon old, proven and beautiful, workable patterns, requires courage, conviction, a great deal of self-confidence. Perhaps women, recognizing that their gender is not so intricately woven into the tradition, not the gender that primarily created the tradition, can be slightly aloof from its pressures, more free than men from its strictures and intimidations and thus more amenable to attempting those daring changes which must be attempted. The views of women, mothers in particular, and their universal perspectives have not been absolutely defined or elucidated by the voices of women in our literary tradition. Women are free, then, in many ways, to originate and shape these definitions themselves now.

The perspectives of women will necessarily be varied and contradictory and their approaches multiple. If there is something called the male perspective in our literary tradition, then the male perspective of the seventeeth century is not the male perspective of the nineteenth or the twentieth. We don't find in the tradition a single, consistent male perspective even within a particular period, and we won't expect to find a consistent female perspective either. But we can expect women's voices to add new insights and new approaches to old questions.

Concerning the evolution of tradition, Eliot states, in his essay "Tradition and the Individual Talent": "The existing monuments form an ideal order among themselves, which is modified by the introduction of the new (the really new) work of art among them." This is the nature of the tradition, its fluidity. The tradition is not a static monolith. It accommodates itself, reshapes, redefines its essence, with the introduction of new works of art. Women's work can play a role in this reshaping process.

The English language, also, is in continual flux. It changes as the investigation of the universe and our perception of our place in it expands and alters. The issues and events of the latter half of the twentieth century are startling and exhilarating. Language as art must keep pace with the discoveries that radically influence the way we see ourselves. The astronomer Frederick Hoyle prophesied that, "Once a photograph of the Earth taken from the outside is available, a new idea as powerful as any in history will be let loose." The explication of this "new idea" is clearly not the sole prerogative of any single voice or perspective, male or female, and the language needed to formulate this"new idea" has no gender. Women and men together will be engaged in the process of shaping the language required to investigate the spiritual questions of our generation.

We're all here now, today, men and women together, all of us sometimes frightened, sometimes bewildered, sometimes delighted, possessing less than a smattering of knowledge, without understanding, perceiving the humor in our ineptitude, struggling, aware of our approaching deaths. Who are we? What are we? Where are we? What are our obligations? These are the crucial questions. Occasionally we glimpse the divine, but we don't know how to secure that vision. The best we can do as a community is to leave for those who come after us the most beautiful record we can produce of our efforts to achieve insight and dignity. All of us in the literary community are in the process of trying to create the literature of our times, what kind of people we were, what kind of people we aspired to be, what we were able to give back for the gifts we received. Whatever strengths I have to work with as a woman I embrace in this effort.

NOTES

1. *Elliott Bay Booknotes*, Elliott Bay Book Co. (Seattle: Summer 1992), p. 1.

2. *American Audio Prose Library Catalog*, 1991-92, p. 18.

THE PERSISTENCE OF TRADITION

Grace Schulman

Tradition has a way of exerting its strongest hold on us when we are least aware of its presence. At times a striking genre, such as the Mayan legend, or the Swahili wedding song, affects us so profoundly that we bear its traces without giving it a name. Harold Bloom writes of that tendency in *Agon: Towards a Theory of Revisionism*. He states: "Unnaming always has been a major mode in poetry, far more than naming; perhaps there cannot be a poetic naming that is not founded on an unnaming."[1]

The process of unnaming intrigues me, for many deep sympathies have no apparent explanation. Recently I finished a poem called "Footsteps on Lower Broadway," in which I identified closely with three nineteenth-century figures: Henry James, Walt Whitman, and my grandfather, a Hungarian-born Jewish immigrant. What bonded the unlikely trio, for me, were their separate but similar predilections for lower New York. At different times, Whitman and my grandfather saw Grace Church steeple as they walked up from the Battery, listened to Italian opera, and heard street shouts of merchants and reformers. Henry James and my grandfather saw the tall buildings I still pass by every day, some of them decorated with stone gargoyles, animals, and griffins.

Since writing the poem, a ballade of ten ten-line stanzas, I have thought continually about the mysterious nature of handing-down. Apart from my affinities for language and for walking in lower New York, I cannot classify the enormous impact those men have had on my life and work.

What intrigues me, though, is the attraction James and Whitman had to the heritage of my grandfather, a man they never knew. For James, that interest is conveyed less in the content than in the vigorous tone of his language. In *The American Scene*, James writes of viewing, at the age of sixty-two, the lower East Side ghetto of European immigrant Jews. My grandfather had moved away years before, first to attend law school and then to establish a practice on lower Broadway. Noting the crowded living conditions, James was appalled but fascinated. He used excited words such as "bristled" and "swarmed." He wrote: "The scene hummed with the human presence beyond any I have ever faced."[2]

For Whitman, the appeal was overwhelming. In March 1842, Whitman, at twenty-three, attended services twice at a synagogue in lower Manhattan, and reported his experiences in leaders he wrote for his newspaper, *The Aurora*. He visited the Shearith Israel Synagogue on Crosby Street, a modest building dwarfed by St. Paul's nearby.

Whitman's account is worth quoting at length, for it is filled with wonder so intense as to show him at a loss for words. The poet who was born of Dutch and English farm folk with Quaker tendencies was new to Jewish ritual. He was dazzled by the ancient forms of worship and by the chants, the more so because he did not comprehend the strange language. His lack of comprehension led to a narrative mode that was simultaneously halting *and* urgent. He wrote:

> The whole scene was entirely new; never had we beheld any thing of a similar description before. The congregation (we don't know what other word to use) were all standing, each one with his hat on . . . . In the middle of the room was a raised platform about four yards square, with heavy balustrade of bronze work and mahogany around it. Upon the centre of this platform was a figure which, by the voice coming from it, we knew to be a man. None of the lineaments of the human form, however, were visible; for one of the large silk mantles alluded to was thrown over his head, and completely shrouded him. He was speaking; but as his language was Hebrew, we could not understand a word he uttered.[3]

Unable to define, or even to name, the sacred Ark that holds the Torah (five books of Moses), Whitman marveled at its part in the service:

. . . At the further end of the room stood an erection very much resembling the front that pictures give the ancient Parthenon. Under it was a semicircular partitioned enclosure, of panelled wood, which from the ornaments and expensive tracery lavished upon the whole affair seemed intended to contain something either very valuable, or very sacred.

It was the Ark he returned to in his second account, again in the tone of uninitiated enchantment, unknowing, unnaming:

After the performance had continued for some time as we described it in yesterday's *Aurora*, some of the Jews went up to the semicircular panel work before mentioned, unlocked it, and opened the doors. Three or four of them took from the inclosure certain contrivances, which we dare hardly pretend to describe, for fear of bungling in the attempt. As near as we can now recollect, they resembled in shape large sugar loaves; and each had an ornamental and fantastic affair made of silver and glass upon its top. These were brought up to the platform in the centre, and each of the silver ornaments we have described was taken from the top of the sugar loaf structure, and put upon the desk in front.

The priest then raised aloft a large scroll of parchment, probably the sacred law—wafting it around so that the people could see it in all parts of the house. All this while he uttered a kind of chant, to which the men and women made responses.

Lacking names, Whitman focused on the imagery, the rhythms, the human involvement. He was transported:

The heart within us felt awed as in the presence of memorials from an age that had passed away centuries ago. The strange and discordant tongue—the mystery, and all the associations that crowded themselves in troops upon our mind—made a thrilling sensation to creep through every nerve. It was indeed a sight well calculated to impress the mind with an unwonted tone.

Enchanted as he was, Whitman did not use the ritual as a topic in his poetry. In his verse, there are no references to the synagogue services and only cursory allusions to Hebrew music. That, in itself, is not more surprising than any poet's omission of an exciting experience. However, it does seem odd that in his great passage concerning world religions, Judaism does not appear. The section beginning "I do not despise you, priests" (*Leaves of Grass*,

Chant 43), includes the priest, the lama and the brahmin, but not the rabbi. And although the Koran and the Gospels are named among the poet's scriptures, the Torah—"the ornamental and fantastic affair" that had charmed him years before—is not.

Nor would the lapse of thirteen years between the *Aurora* leaders and the first publication of *Leaves of Grass* explain the omission of Judaism from the poetry. Whitman incorporated much that was contemporaneous with the synagogue ritual: the contralto in the organ loft, the omnibus drivers, "the blab of the pave," "the vault at Pfaff's." And even if, in the interim, he was attracted far more to other Eastern philosophies, he was a poet who gathered in and contained ideas simultaneously, rather than moving from one to another.

From the newspaper account, I would surmise that his exclusion had to do with the impossibility of examining what he could not name. The poet who wrote "all truths wait in things" studied identifiable objects that embodied the spirit. In the Jewish services, he found truths without things he could identify, or the unearthly "journeywork of the stars" without its earthly equivalent, the "leaves of grass" drawing the mind toward the celestial.

Actually, Judaism is fundamental to Whitman's verse, but in a more subtle way. A clue to the poet's practice is in his prose, a later (1888) essay called "The Bible as Poetry," first collected in *November Boughs*. Here he lauds the Hebrew poets for their bold figurative language, and for their concerns with vital emotions:

> The metaphors daring beyond account, the lawless soul, extravagant by our standards, the glow of love and friendship, the fervent kiss—nothing in argument or logic, but unsurpass'd in proverbs, in religious ecstasy, in suggestions of common mortality and death, man's great equalizers—the spirit everything, the ceremonies and forms of the churches nothing, faith limitless, its immense sensuousness immensely spiritual—an incredible, all-inclusive non-worldliness and dew-scented illiteracy (the antipodes of our Nineteenth Century business absorption and morbid refinement)—no hair-splitting doubts, no sickly sulking and sniffling, no "hamlet," no "Adonais," no "Thanatopsis," no "In Memoriam."[4]

What Whitman said he admired in Hebrew poetry he had consecrated in his own verse years before. "Logic and sermons do not convince," he asserts in *Leaves of Grass*, just as, throughout his verse, he celebrates the spirit and its companion, sensuousness, over the church.

More significant, though, is his musical affinity to the Hebrew bible. In his biography, *Walt Whitman: A Life*, Justin Kaplan writes that in the poet's religious education at St. Ann's Episcopal and at the Dutch Reformed Church, "he was duly instructed in Scripture and catechism, but what remained with him was the Bible's rhythm and imagery. . . ."[5] The magnificent long sentence quoted above from Whitman's essay, "The Bible as Poetry," is in an acervate style, its amassment and reiteration of detail focusing attention on the writer's process of thought. That manner of listing is prominent in the Hebrew bible as well as in Whitman's poetry.

And, of course, Whitman follows the Hebrew bible in his recurrent uses of anaphora:

> All spheres, grown, ungrown, small, large, suns, moons, planets,
> All distances of place however wide,
> All distances of time, all inanimate forms . . .

and parallelism:

> Forests at the bottom of the sea, the branches and leaves . . .
> (Both passages from "Sea-Drift")

And besides the poetic devices, entire structural concepts from the Hebrew bible made their way into Whitman's verse. The rhythmic divisions of, for example, the Song of Songs, whose chapters are sequences of verse modulated from theme to theme, one image suggesting another, are analogous to the chants in *Leaves of Grass*.

What the poet was unable to identify, he was unable to exclude. Whitman's youthful fondness for biblical rhythm was sharpened by the odd synagogue chants in the "strange and discordant tongue," the music that was to inform his own.

As it was with Whitman, it is with us all. We are carriers of images from countless cultures, some of which are unknown to us, some seemingly remote. Only in part are we shaped by writers we acclaim, for influences live in the unconscious. There are, in fact, mysterious transmissions of information between cultures that are far apart in time and space. The late Willard Trask, a major translator, offers an example: he observes that medieval Galician and Portuguese poets cultivated a genre called "the girl's song" that was similar in form—rhyme scheme, meter, and line recurrences— to songs in China of the sixth century B.C.E.[6] We know from "Songs of Cifar," the modern Nicaraguan epic by Pablo Antonio Cuadra, that folklore of his native country contains archetypes and images with resemblances to those crafted by Homer and Lycophron. Some theorists speculate that astonishing cultural exchanges are based on rare but actual contacts, usually through commerce. However, I suspect they have causes that are less circumstantial, based on common emotions and universal celebrations.

In his 1919 essay, "Tradition and the Individual Talent," T. S. Eliot asserts: "The existing monuments form an ideal order among themselves, which is modified by the introduction of the new (the really new) work of art among them." He assumes a reciprocal process: Just as art of the past influences the present, the artist of the present transforms the past by assimilation.

Today, more than ever, we find literature a continuum, with every work of art related to every other. In fact, where Eliot wrote of "traditions"—referring, for example, to the metaphysicals, or the Elizabethans—I would extend his observation to say there are many cultures, but only one tradition. One vast tradition comprises black, white, Asian, woman, man, Christian, Jew, Moslem, Buddhist. It contains works of conflicting aesthetic persuasions, all "modifying" one another, to use Eliot's term, and all available in our bookstores, concert halls, and galleries.

As I write this now, I am surrounded by cultures, all of them beautiful. Without getting up from my desk I can see, on the shelves around me, a new translation of the *Gilgamesh*, by David Ferry; an anthology of Chinese poetry edited by Donald Finkel; Lu Chi's *Wen Fu*, a new translation by Sam Hamill; William Matthews' versions of Martial in his *Selected Poems and Translations*; anthologies of Russian poetry and of African poetry; and a programme from the Barbican Theatre in London, for Sophocles' Theban trilogy in a new translation by Timberlake Wertenbaker, and with choric dances that include, appropriately, African and Asian dances that may have informed ancient drama.

I caught those books at a glance, and I'm sure I omitted many, perhaps those most important to me. That is, I excluded their names, but not their importance to me. As I've said, Whitman praised Judaism not by naming it in his poems but by incorporating the rhythms of its liturgy; Henry James honored Jewish immigrants in his prose, not in the content but in the vigorous language. So too, those unnamed books are luminous questions in my mind. The less I am aware of their implications, the larger they grow. However I may wish to, I cannot exclude even those that seem remote from my own life and art. They are alive in me, and they will not be silent.

NOTES

1. Harold Bloom, *Agon: Towards a Theory of Revisionism* (New York: Oxford U. Press, 1983), p. 181.

2. Henry James, *The American Scene* (New York: Simon and Schuster, 1906), p. 131.

3. Walt Whitman, *Walt Whitman at the New York Aurora, Editor at 22: A Collection of Recently Discovered Writings*, ed. Joseph Jay Rubin and Charles H. Brown (State College, Pa.: Bald Eagle Press, 1950). All citations here are to pp. 31-33.

4. Walt Whitman, *Rivulets of Prose: Critical Essays*, ed. Carolyn Wells and Alfred Goldsmith (Freeport, N. Y.: Books for Libraries Press,1969), pp. 47-48.

5. Justin Kaplan, *Walt Whitman: A Life* (New York: Simon and Schuster, 1980), p. 70.

6. Willard Trask, "King Denis of Portugal," in *Translation VI* (Winter 1978-79), pp. 10-11.

All direct citations to Whitman's poetry are to the following: *Walt Whitman's Leaves of Grass: The First (1855) Edition,* ed. Malcolm Cowley (New York: The Viking Press, 1967); and *Walt Whitman, Leaves of Grass: Comprehensive Reader's Edition,* ed. Harold W. Blodgett and Scully Bradley (New York: Norton, 1965).

SOME OBSERVATIONS ON WOMEN AND TRADITION

Anne Stevenson

You have asked me to comment on my feelings about what you see as a predominantly male tradition in English and American literature. Citing a passage from T. S. Eliot's essay, "Tradition and the Individual Talent," you specifically ask if, as a woman writer, I feel left out. My answer is no, I do not. The question appears to me to lie quite outside the issues Eliot addressed in that essay. Moreover, although anyone can see that women have had a tough time finding acceptance in almost all other professions and fields of study, it seems to me difficult to prove by example that for two hundred years women have not held their own as writers, particularly as writers of fiction. To that I will come later. But first of all, suppose we look closely at Eliot's essay and the terms it employs.

"Tradition," as used in literary criticism, appears to be a word that emerged late, under pressure of modern usage. Eliot himself introduced it in the twenties out of a new and heightened consciousness of poetry's historical lineage. The essay in question begins cautiously: "In English writing we seldom speak of tradition, though we occasionally apply its name in deploring its absence." He seems to be identifying a point of view, a state of affairs that may not objectively exist. "Seldom, perhaps," he goes on, "does the word appear except in a phrase of censure." The *Oxford English Dictionary* offers no examples of literary tradition. An old word derived from the Latin *traditio-onem*, it seems to have ecclesiastical roots, a transmission or handing down of rules and ceremonies in the church. A further definition (4) gives "the action of transmitting. . . from one to another, or from generation to generation. . . beliefs, rules, customs, or the like, esp. by word of mouth or *by practice without writing*."

"Tradition," in a traditional sense, then, would seem to apply chiefly to undefined custom. It may be a term that does not ask to be made explicit until it provokes opposition. When writings naturally belong to a tradition—as Shakespeare's plays and sonnets belong to the Elizabethan period, and Jane Austen's prose reflects the accepted style of the eighteenth century—no reason arises to label writers "traditional" as such. The notion of rebelling against a norm and defying tradition can be traced back to the English Reformation's reaction against the Catholic church. Milton coupled the word with the equally frowned upon "superstition" in *Paradise Lost*: "and the truth/ With superstitions and traditions taint" (XII, l. 512).

Be that as it may, Eliot, and F. R. Leavis after him, found the concept of a tradition indispensable to their literary polemic. It is easy to see—easier now than when Eliot was writing—that "Tradition and the Individual Talent" is constructed primarily as a defense. After World War I, Eliot (rightly) anticipated the disintegration of an aesthetic inheritance he held to be particularly precious. His personal desire to salvage what he called "the historical sense" led him to define tradition in such a way as to preserve what he saw as valuable in the past while giving himself full license to forge ahead with literary experiment. It seems, then, that this essay by a poet famous for his insistence on the impersonality of the artist can be read as an intensely personal plea. At its heart is a statement of the central time-motif of *Four Quartets*:

> . . . the historical sense involves a perception, not only of the pastness of the past, but of its presence; the historical sense compels a man to write not merely with his own generation in his bones, but with a feeling that the whole of the literature of Europe from Homer and within it the whole of the literature of his own country has a simultaneous existence and composes a simultaneous order. This historical sense, which is a sense of the timeless as well as of the temporal and of the timeless and of the temporal together, is what makes a writer traditional. And it is at the same time what makes a writer most acutely conscious of his place in time, of his contemporaneity. (p. 38)

Whatever you make of "time present and time past. . . both perhaps present in time future," it must be allowed that the exclusion of women had no part in the poet's view. Indeed, it would never have crossed Eliot's mind that a body of feminists in the late years of this extraordinary century might take offense. Nor, it seems to me, would he have considered the fourteenth-century anchoress Julian of Norwich, quoted in the third part of "Little Gidding," to be in any way isolated from the tradition because she was a "woman mystic." Surely, the plane on which Eliot conceived of poetry, like it or not, had nothing to do with today's political scuffling between the sexes; and if women writers feel excluded from what they read into his meaning, it seems to me that they are misjudging a *literary* essay written by a particular man at a particular time, in order to make out, in quite another time, a *political* case for initiating a tradition of their own.

Many people would argue, of course, that there is no literature that is not also political, and that may be something of what Eliot meant by "the historical sense"—the carrying back of the literary imagination into the social and political past. I would question, however, the legitimacy of searching through his "text" like self-appointed members of a thought-police for proof that "patriarchy" lay at the root of Eliot's criticism all along; that his use of the masculine noun and pronouns "man" and "his" gives him away; that his whole mode of discourse disregards woman's just cause for resentment after ages of cultural exclusion. By now critics have got used to the equalizing terminology of Marxist theory (or perhaps I should say "cultural materialism"); and we also hear— thanks to a somewhat surprising injection of Freud into feminist theory—a great deal about subliminal discrimination and the unconscious prejudice of language. To me such arguments only offer more proof of postmodernism's lamentable tendency to bundle up social and psychological perceptions into ideological sandbags and then employ them in argument as if they were the building blocks of some ultimate social (and of course prescriptively moral) enlightenment.

Poor old Eliot, poor old Dr. Leavis. The literary values they sought to establish—aesthetic, moral, and historical, but not in any way designed to promote sexual discrimination (Leavis championed two women novelists out of four in his *Great Tradition*)—have been smashed to smithereens in less than fifty years of bullying ideology. To be sure, men, if we want to consider them as a class of beings distinct and opposed to women (which I do not), are more accustomed than we are to raising abstract ideas to a plane of eminence. Since civilization began, male thinkers have taken responsibility for humanity's quest for truth and meaning; it is a truism of history that in general women have employed themselves more practically. All the more reason, one would have thought, for the application on women's part of a little refreshing skepticism. How much academic clout and sense of importance the theorizing men of the twentieth century have attracted to themselves, with their tedious -isms and -ologies. How much power they have wielded, how many trees have been sacrificed to bring out their unreadable books!

And women, meanwhile? How have women writers and feminist critics, as a body, responded over the past forty years to this intimidating, jargon-studded blitz? Instead of splitting our sides with laughter, or, more to the point, polishing the art of exact perception and drawing on the wit, wisdom, good sense, and deep suspicion of display we have inherited from our own branch of the English literary tree—beginning with Jane Austen and continuing right up through Gertrude Stein, Carson McCullers, and Elizabeth Bishop—we have hurried around in a panic looking for ways to adapt the jargon of these over-serious and ridiculously pompous men to our own sectarian and mainly self-justifying purposes.

What a situation! As if literary criticism were a more impressive and admirable profession than the writing of literature at first hand. How much easier, how much grander, how much more lucrative it is to establish a system of categories and caveats than to incur the aesthetic and financial risks of writing poetry or fiction oneself. No wonder some critics have done their best to abolish the concept of the author. The idea that the "culture" is responsible for producing a poem or a novel makes it possible for a critic, in the name of that abstract concept, to claim credit as a co-creator.

This is not to say that all literary criticism is worthless. The response and considered opinion of any informed outsider honestly and passionately engaged in the text can be immensely helpful to a reader. Writers themselves are critics. I can see, for instance, how important it was for Eliot, *as a poet*, to postulate an "ideal order" of literary "monuments" without either much liking his choice of noun—"monuments" is too cold and museum-like to be anything like the right image for poetry—or agreeing with him in the narrow exclusiveness of his tastes. I find his essay illuminating, nevertheless, as much for what it teaches me about the self-consciousness serious writers of his generation introduced into criticism as for what it says about self-sacrifice and the extinction of the poet's personality. Ironically, it's that self-consciousness or "acute consciousness" that a writer should have, according to Eliot, of his "place in time" that above all appears to be modernism's legacy to the present.

Young American women of my generation (I graduated from the University of Michigan in 1954) listened to Eliot, Leavis, and the fathers of the New Criticism because they taught us not only *what* was important to read, but *how* to read; how, that is, to pay close attention to words, how to look for what was good or bad, convincing or weak in writing. It's that *how* that stays with me as the most valuable lesson of my college years, and not the *who* or *what* of anyone's prescriptive theory. I still believe that the rereadability of a book—outside of its time—secures it a place in tradition, and not the sex of its author or its moral value as "truth"—especially if you regard as "true" the sacred-sounding terminology of evangelical feminism.

Given my perspective, you can see why, in my view, it matters hardly at all whether the books history has shown to be rereadable—loved over many generations of readers—were written by men or by women. I don't say differences don't exist. No reader could fail to see, say, that Fielding's full-blooded social range was not available to Jane Austen. Who, though, was the finer writer? As the nineteenth-century wore on, women's writing engaged with a larger social spectrum; and in our own permissive time, women have as much access to public folly as men. As human beings, we are all flawed, wrong, sorry, tragic and comic, guided and influenced by each other, subject to the temptations of vanity, worldliness and all the assorted ills of nature. That is the human condition "traditional" writing engages with, and it shines in a recognizable form through all literature worth reading.

Writers like Virginia Woolf, contemporary with Eliot and incensed at their exclusion from what they increasingly understood to be a man's world, quite rightly made a fuss about being left out and maintained on the margins of power. All honor to them. Today the male establishment is being persuaded into accepting the justice of sharing power with women. The question that arises is whether women, especially women writers, are going to like it. For a writer it is generally an advantage to be free of power, free of responsibility for anonymous others and from the necessity of making a living. When I began to write I believed that taking a job in publishing or teaching would stimulate me to produce. I soon found I had no energy to write after a day's work, especially as I had to attend to the needs of my children when I came home. How fortunate Emily Dickinson had been, I thought, in her dependent seclusion. Virginia Woolf was, in this respect, equally privileged. In the past, many women writers, for obvious reasons, decided (or had the decision thrust upon them) not to marry and have children. Thanks to contraception, it is easy today to choose sex without children, but are women writers any better—or happier?

One of the ways in which women's greater freedom in society has affected us all—men as well as women—is that, in intellectual circles anyway, the stereotype of man-at-work, woman-at-home has been broken. No longer is it shameful for men to stay at home or for a woman to support a man, should the man be the working artist. Many happy arrangements of this kind exist among my friends, although significantly in most cases, it is the man who has gratefully accepted liberation by his working wife. I see no reason why a women writer should not equally accept support from her husband or partner—although if she were serious about feminism, it might be difficult for her not to regard her exclusion from worldly power as a reversion to old patterns.

My feeling is generally that, given a modicum of time and money, women writers are now—as individuals, and to hell with a conglomerate women's tradition—neither better nor worse off than they were a hundred years ago. Perhaps it was easier then. No one told Miss Austen or Miss Dickinson or Mrs. Gaskell or Mrs. Humphrey Ward that they ought to be on the lookout for dimensions of women's collective psyche. Being unencumbered by theory, they wrote, one assumes, because they were good at it. Or because writing brought them money, friends, and fame. Some women poets were eccentric—but then so were men poets. Nineteenth-century society may have ignored spinster daughters, turned its back on genius, and taken stupid writers to heart, but that is no more than happens today. Such discrimination as we notice from the perspective of the nineties is likely to be warped by our predisposition to see all women writers up to and including Sylvia Plath as victims of the patriarchal system. I don't believe, however, that a comparison of the greatest men of the time would result in a higher rate of contemporary success for men: think of Blake, Keats, Clare, and Gerard Hopkins.

The truth is that, in all ways that matter, what goes for men goes for women. The best writing can't be forced. It usually can't be taken up, nine to five, like a profession. It is a "process"—Eliot's word again—that the true writer of whatever sex or class learns to manage in the face of constant failure and frustration. The challenge that "reality," in all its confusion and complexity, presents to the human instinct to catch it, or transform it, or touch something important in language, is only rarely rewarded by a feeling of achievement. Above all, writing fiction or poetry (the term "creative writing" is again contemporary jargon) means absorption in a self-enclosed, self-delighting imagination. Whether a self-serving critical establishment, male or female, approves of it or not is no concern of the writer's. When a poet or novelist is "really writing" as Sylvia Plath put it—slipping perhaps into sudden ease after a long struggle with the extraneous—then the whole labelling apparatus of criticism, ideology, power struggle, and self-consciousness become blissfully irrelevant. The fate of any piece of imaginative writing—not a "text"—ultimately depends on an indefinable line of sympathy (tradition) that it establishes with future human readers. It is they who will ultimately determine whether it lives or dies.

Postscript

I am conscious that what I have written about women and the tradition pretty exclusively addresses itself to modern literature, particularly to what I would consider to be the best, or most rereadable literature of the past two hundred years. I recognize, of course, that there is a social dimension to any aesthetic consideration; and it is a truism to say that before the advent of the novel (a form that chiefly arose in response to the tastes and demands of lady readers) women had virtually no chance at all publicly to develop their talents.

Anne Stevenson 181

To return to the social dimension: I am more than ready to admit that inequalities of opportunity still exist, although these, as I see them, often pertain to the nature of the sexual relation, whatever the culture. I don't see how sexual attraction, sexual jealousy, and the tendency of men and women in strange situations to stick together as groups can be legislated away. Perhaps this example from my own experience will illustrate what I mean.

In my last year as writer-in-residence at the University of Edinburgh, I attended a poetry reading given by two distinguished European poets, one of whose work I admired very much. I looked forward to talking to this poet after the reading about poetry, favorite poets and so forth, but unfortunately, he had come to Edinburgh with his wife—an attractive woman without intellectual pretensions—and over drinks in the staff club I became aware that they both were apprehensive of advances to him by other women. As hostess of the party, I felt obliged to make people comfortable (a man might have felt the same, but it would have been easy for him to sit down with the men) so I immediately introduced myself to the wife. We sat down with a number of other women—mainly academics—while the men gathered at the bar. I don't remember a more frustrating evening. We women talked about children and women's work outside the family, the pleasures of travel, what to see in Edinburgh, but we said not a word about poetry except to praise the reading generally. All this time, I confess, I kept casting my eyes at the circle of men who, with Norman MacCaig in their midst and the European poets eagerly questioning him, were happily engaged in literary discussion. Over near the bar the whiskey flowed amid loud bursts of laughter. In our discreet corner, the wife, struggling to speak English between sips of wine, held us in excruciating bondage.

Had I been less polite and more aggressive (by nature or training?), or less sensitive to what both the poet and his wife seemed to desire, I would have made an offer of second drinks an excuse to leave the women and join the poets. Yet that very initiative on my part (or so I believed) would have drawn attention to me, not as a poet but as a discontented woman bent on forcing a man to notice her. Had I insisted on breaking in on the men's circle, I would have spoiled their talk, injured the feelings of the poet's wife, and worst of all, made the possibility of talking to the poet at some future time all but impossible. So I stayed where I was and very shortly made an excuse to go home.

Later I made a note about the evening in my diary, thinking that someday it might be the seed of a story or a chapter in a novel. Perhaps it will. Such slight, memorable human situations are the stuff of fiction. The first rule for a writer is to remain detached; and never to attribute particular, unavoidable discomforts to the workings of some inexorable cultural law.

NOTES

This essay was also published in England, in *PN/Review* 87, Vol. 19, No.1 (Sept./Oct. 1992), pp. 25-28.

TERRIBLE PERFECTION: IN THE FACE OF TRADITION

Deborah Tall

"Perfection is terrible, it cannot have children." The opening lines of Sylvia Plath's "The Munich Mannequins" chilled me with unexpected insight and unleashed the long process of grappling with who I would be as a writer. Perfection, in Plath's poem, is the sterility of self-absorbed love, imagistically evoked in the "sulphur loveliness" of mannequins propping up furs in a lace-trimmed shop window. It is "cold as snow breath," "intolerable," "voiceless."

For some reason, even when I was a pre-feminist adolescent, that word "perfection" sent out menacing ripples in several directions—I immediately attached it to a masculine ideal and extended it to the notion of the perfect poem, that formally crafted, correctly proportioned and modulated, male poem. What had drawn me first to poetry had been the sexy wordplay of e. e. cummings and the boldness of Plath, but unhappily, my "official" education up to that point had led me to the unfortunate conclusion that what was truly "literary" was, rather, as sterile as Plath's mannequins, elaborately artificial, polite, "masked" from any authentic expression of human experience. I wasn't the only one in such a bind. After all, the greatest insult one could hurl or receive in a student poetry workshop in the late sixties, awash in the politics of free verse, was that a line or image was too "poetic" or "literary."

I wasn't alone, either, in my general suspicion of perfection. Listen to Tennyson on the subject: "Faultily faultless, icily regular, splendidly null/Dead perfection, no more." To be perfect was to have stopped changing, to die, to be anthologized. "The woman is perfected/Her dead/Body wears the smile of accomplishment," as Plath has it in the final poem before her suicide. Such accomplishment in a poem stood, in my mind, for the very opposite of life—especially sex and domestic life. To live an expansive, many-faceted life would no doubt mean risking numerous imperfections; not to live such a life risked the reduction of experience, freeze drying.

And yet, there was approved and perfect literature on all the reading lists, held up as challenge. If I wanted to be a poet, I supposed I would have to strive toward "terrible" perfection as an ideal, but early on I sensed that I could achieve it only at the cost of—among other things—a family ("it cannot have children"). Maybe Yeats was right, and one had to choose between the perfection of the life and of the work. But did I, anyway, want "perfection" as defined by others? The poets I loved best were eccentric or even mad; their poems admitted a certain messiness. So I armed myself with those like Zola who boasted: "I am little concerned with beauty or perfection. I don't care for the great centuries. All I care about is life, struggle, intensity. I am at ease in my generation."

Despite my ahistorical cockiness, Plath's mannequins struck at the heart of my emerging ambition and fear as a woman. Of course I had inherited a highly romantic, male notion of the artist, a being untethered by domestic concerns, but I didn't know that yet. I didn't know there were alternatives. All I knew was that the two poets I prized most, who had made the act of continuing to write even seem possible—Plath and Adrienne Rich—had both reacted with ambivalence (to say the least) to being wives and mothers. While their passionate intelligence and verbal music fed me, they didn't offer much reassurance on that thorny subject. I was still more susceptible, finally, to the grisly romance of James Wright, for instance, elegizing his suicide-muse, Jenny, "sleeping down there / Face down in the unbelievable silk of spring"—

> Come up to me love,
> Out of the river, or I will
> Come down to you.[1]

Singing to the muse at the edge of an abyss seemed easier, at that point, than figuring out how to live as a woman poet.

Not surprisingly, then, I opted for high romance in my personal life as a way to numb my fears. I fell in love with an Irish writer twenty years my senior and went off, in 1972, to live with him on a

Deborah Tall   185 &

remote Irish island. The Irishman fit my inherited model of the writer well—he was charismatic, opinionated, rebellious, confident to the point of arrogance, a purist about his writing. I tried, thinly, to remake myself in his guise, while at the same time I inserted myself predictably into the life he shaped for us—becoming his typist as well as his cook and lover. Definitely the junior partner, I set up a table in the bedroom of the stone cottage while he got the desk in the spare room. Between chores, I worked on poems.

"What you must always do, my dear," Elizabeth Gaskell once advised a young woman hoping to become a writer (my ears perked up), "is put the dinner on in the morning and soak the laundry overnight." This over the radio one day shortly after I had settled in rural Ireland, and was overwhelmed by the physical burden of each day's necessary struggle for food, warmth, and water. "You damn well better get organized if you expect to accomplish anything," was the message I heard—and the tip about the laundry in a world without washing machines was dead on. I had to laugh. There I was, another aspiring woman writer caught in a centuries-old dilemma, directed toward her own energies by a legacy of practical experience, given the courage to demand a block of silence in the middle of each day.

We were living on subsistence farming and fishing and a bit of freelance writing. Though our living conditions were stringent, with careful planning I could spend a good part of the day writing poems. I felt a sense of noble mission and a blessed reprieve from dull, work-a-day American life. I was blessed, too, in being surrounded by a lively, verbal peasant community that prized writers. I learned discipline and silence, the rhythm of a pure writing life. When a London publisher accepted my first book of poems, I felt I had actually achieved something close to my notion of the writer's life.

It was only when I began having modest success with my writing that the tensions in our domestic arrangements showed. I was no longer the idolizing student, unquestioningly grateful for validation and the key to adult literary life, but a genuine fellow writer needing to find her place in her own world. After five years our relationship broke, and I returned to the United States.

Though I knew I had to face the music and make a life for myself here, I still hadn't learned much. I'd missed the era of consciousness-raising while salting fish in Ireland. In my reading, I'd found other women poets to fall in love with—Tsvetaeva and Akhmatova especially—but they had lived *in extremis*, hardly offering me a model of the life I was going to have to confront back in New York City in the late seventies. And what about American poetry? Didn't I have to take my place in *it*?

*

When I was an undergraduate, the edifice of poetic tradition—both American and English—had more or less repelled me. It reeked of footnotes. Tradition was defined by *The Norton Anthology*. I far too often skipped literature classes to stay alone in the dorm room and write. But fortunately, at the University of Michigan in the late sixties and early seventies, there was a live literary alternative in the form of numerous poetry readings and workshops. And my mentor, Donald Hall, was an extraordinarily generous teacher. The bulk of my education took place in his living room, during the casual dinners he gave for visiting poets. Most crucially, he gave us students the gift of being taken seriously, and through his light touch, the impetus to work hard independently.

When I read Hall's essays on poetics years later, though, I was surprised to discover how much more he knew than what he'd disseminated in class. Maybe I hadn't been listening carefully enough. Maybe he knew we weren't up to it, that we were better off discovering certain things on our own. But I think what's truer is that most of my generation were taught by poets who had successfully broken the stranglehold of literary tradition and what they passed on to us most palpably was their rebelliousness and sense of liberation—even though they themselves thoroughly knew and still loved much of the tradition they had been taught. So while Donald Hall, for example, shows an impressively astute understanding of rhythm and meter in his essays and his own poems, I don't recall his ever having taught us a metrical poem. What I most vitally inherited, then, was not the canon itself, but a stance *against* it. We read Wright, Merwin, and others who had begun by writing in meter and (wisely, we concurred) given it up. I skimmed those early poems. Robert Bly came to Ann Arbor annually to reinforce the message we were happily absorbing. The "deep image" and the rejection of American and English poetry for South American and European fit our Vietnam-era politics and our underdeveloped ears well. Tradition, as I understood it then, was an irrelevance to me, and it took a long time until I could return to the canon without feeling withered by the weight of its status or simply alienated.

Years later, preparing to teach the *Odyssey* for the first time, I came upon C. S. Lewis's comment that:

> Every poem has two parents—its mother being the mass of experience, thought, and the like, inside the poet, and its father the pre-existing form (epic, tragedy, the novel, or what not) which he meets in the public world. . . . It is easy to forget that the man who writes a good love sonnet needs not only to be enamoured of a woman, but also to be enamoured of the sonnet.[2]

I knew, with embarrassment, that it was something like the truth (despite its gendering), and that my poems weren't going to develop as I wanted them to if I didn't take stock, discover who all my invisible influences had been, find which poets stood behind the rebellious poets I had been reared on.

I returned to the masters, not out of obligation this time, but with genuine curiosity, and a firmer sense of what I was looking for. I knew by then that if we owe literary tradition anything, it's our conscious revision of it, the accumulation of human attention. Eliot, of course, argues in "Tradition and the Individual Talent" that we shape the literary past with new work just as it shapes us. He'd probably be shocked, though, to see how extensively we've applied that principle in recent decades. His confidence in the knowable entity of the "whole" of literature inevitably feels quaint to us now. We have so opened up the definition of literary tradition that it will never again fit in a single anthology (as Norton has now recognized, issuing multiple perspectives on the canon).

The problem with what Eliot propounds, too, is how narrow a concept of tradition it assumes—the certitude that new literature derives from and takes its place among existing literature, period. No poet lives on poetry alone, and the whole of our experience sits with us at the desk. How can we leave out of tradition the other arts, our ethnic and religious traditions, our social status, our inherited gender roles, the place of the arts in our communities, and so on? All of that is as much a part of our tradition, our sense of poetry and its role, as the work of a string of past poets. What a strong, singular sense of literary tradition can do, in fact, if we take it too seriously to the desk, is *exclude*—it has, for instance, until recently (despite Wordsworth and Whitman) encouraged us to edit out "inappropriate" experiences and the colloquial. It can also impose conventional shapes on our not-yet-formed impulses. So while the body of poetry we've read inevitably determines our sense of what a poem can be, other factors can be just as influential—and so is the choice *not* to read certain poets attentively.

I am of the generation that more or less eluded the constrictive aspects of tradition. I have, instead, sometimes felt uneasy about *not* feeling the pressure of tradition, for not caring as deeply as I imagine I should about the last five centuries of English poetry. The explosiveness of American poetry in the past forty years has blasted doorways into so many possibilities that I've felt, for the most part, perfectly entitled to pursue an idiosyncratic path of reading, to find touchstones worldwide.

I've been inspired and consoled over the years by the voices of many women, but also by the voices of men on the margin—the poor, exiled, oppressed—those who, even if they made the canon, ill-fit their world in some revealing way. In the stance of outsiders, I find a corollary to my own relation to the mainstream—as a woman, as a Jew, as a mere second generation American, as a poet in a country and time with little patience for poetry.

I once asked Irish poet Eavan Boland whether Patrick Kavanagh, the unconventional Irish peasant poet, had helped her as a woman writer in a tradition pretty much devoid of women. She answered in terms similar to mine. Kavanagh had been a crucial guide, she said, because of "his fierce attachment to the devalued parts of his experience and a sense of the meaning of that devaluation within a society." Kavanagh made poetry of hay and potatoes; in a sense he gave her "permission" to make poetry of the life inside kitchens and backyards.

But Boland also warns that we must always be aware of what didn't even make it to the *edges* of literature. For the woman writer, Boland says—

> When she looks at what has been written by men and what prevails by men, she is looking at what is *in* the literature. The greater value for women as writers may be their need to be conscious of what is *outside* literature, not just what laps at the shores of literature, but what that literature could not afford to let in. A lot of that is the suffering which lies so much this side of futility that literature would have found it very hard to make sense of.[3]

As writers, we select from the tradition—and from outside it—what we need to nourish us. For many women, that process has been more difficult than for men: the strands of tradition we seek will turn up in unlikely places, out of print, in unheard-of poets. They will often turn up in translation, in the thrill of discovering the unpretentious, clear vision of someone like contemporary Polish poet Wislawa Szymborska ("I prefer myself liking people/to myself loving mankind") or the raw, assertive passion of Finnish poet Edith Södergran in the 1916 poem "We Women":

> We women, we are so close to the brown earth.
> We ask the cuckoo what he expects of spring,
> we embrace the rugged fir tree,
> we look in the sunset for signs and counsel.
> Once I loved a man, he believed in nothing . . .
> He came on a cold day with empty eyes,
> he left on a heavy day with lost memories on his brow.
> If my child does not live, it is his . . .[4]

At such moments we know ourselves part of a great chorus of voices, but not the one to which we were first pointed. The aroused desire to be part of a chorus, though, validates the importance of a historical sense, of tradition; the problem was the narrowness of the tradition we inherited, and the reverence with which it was spoken of.

On the other hand, I doubt that many of us in fact feel quite choral while at the solitude of the desk. Those more ideological in their work than I am may well feel a communal tie even in their most private moments. For me, like others, the lyrical moment is often an escape from the language and issues that dominate my daylight world, a retreat into what doesn't otherwise get said. It is the inchoate, almost inexpressible. And though another's poetry may sometimes spur me to write, often, in its first urges, writing a poem is an escape from literature, a turning away from all the other ways such feelings have already been said—because they don't seem adequate, they aren't the right words for *my* perception, in my time and place. When I'm in the grip of my individual experience, I may succumb to the naïveté of feeling "unique." It is only when I "wake up," a few hours or days out of the poem, that I see its familiarities (even, sometimes, its clichés and stereotypes), how much a poem of my generation or class or sex it is, how it is like other poems as much as it is distinct. It is then that I can "place" it, see its influences, see it in relation to other poets I value. With that consciousness, I can more intelligently revise. For instance, it is useful to recognize that I've emulated Ellen Bryant Voigt in a poem about my daughter, to look back at her work and see how she managed what I'm still struggling with. And it's useful to spot weaknesses through emulation, too—how the excesses of a poet have passed into my poem as shrillness, to reevaluate that poet and her influence. Maybe she slips a notch in my estimation then. Maybe I take her off next year's syllabus for my poetry class. Writing, we revise our private canon continually.

*

Turning outside of strictly literary tradition, I've found crucial guidance in many places. For instance, an essay by anthropologist Keith Basso describing the storytelling of the Western Apache, the courtesy with which speakers treat each other in conversation, seems to me the most convincing case I've ever read for the power of understatement:

> A person who speaks too much—someone who describes too busily, who supplies too many details, who repeats and qualifies too many times—presumes without warrant on the right of hearers to build freely and creatively on the speaker's own depictions. With too many words, such a speaker acts to "smother". . . his or her audience by seeming to say, arrogantly and coercively, "I *demand* that you see everything that happened, how it happened, and why it happened, *exactly* as I do." In other words, persons who speak too much insult the imaginative capabilities of other

people, "blocking their thinking," as one of my consultants put it in English, and "holding down their minds.". . . An effective narrator, they say, takes steps to "open up thinking," thereby encouraging his or her listeners to "travel in their minds."[5]

What better way to describe the give and take of writer and reader? It's inconsiderate, insulting, to overwrite. I'm indebted to a culture that thinks this way. I feel more confident turning away from the body of poetry we're supposed to esteem. I want a poem that reaches out past self-assertive opinion, a poem that holds up experience to the light, lets me see. Reading about the Apache helps me to write such a poem.

Other voices over the years:

Margaret Atwood, at a reading, asked about a woman writer having children, advises: not until you've published your first book, so you *know* you are a writer, and then only one child. (I wait until the second book is out.) When I am pregnant with my second daughter, a feminist friend from New York City says: "You know, they say the second child is a luxury."

Eavan Boland: "In a house with small children, with no time to waste, I gradually reformed my working habits. I learned that if I could not write a poem I could make an image; and if I could not make an image I could take out a word, savor it and store it."[6]

Liz Rosenberg, in a published journal: "The peaceful, even sound of Eli's breathing fills the car. This is my work time, while he naps, but I know if I bring him upstairs he'll wake up and probably not get back to sleep again."[7]

I learn: always carry a notebook, never move a sleeping child, always be ready at a moment's notice to sit down and write, for twenty or forty-five minutes, or a blessed two hours. No standing on ceremony anymore. No prima donna demands for a window with a view and perfect quiet. And then bearing interruption after interruption.

Ellen Bryant Voigt, in my early days of parenthood: "You learn to be very patient." And I see by the gaps between books that she was, and now, her children grown, how many rich poems tumble from her. I write: "Like water become tea through leaves and patience, I can trust myself to this long steeping."

*

My return from rural Ireland in the late seventies demanded a large shift in my conception of myself as poet. Suddenly urban, working on an M.F.A., and then married to a poet of my own generation, struggling to establish a teaching career, having children—headlong I began to do it all, adapting the writing life as I went along. In Ireland I had been literally marginal—on the far western edge of Europe, on the edge of the economy. Now I had one toe in the mainstream, and like so many women of my generation I suddenly found myself welcomed in—to jobs, editors' offices, readings. There was a space in American literary life for women poets; we were in fact revising its character and shape.

But as we enter the center, what of our temperamental affiliation with the edge? Does the writing change, and the relation to literary tradition? Some good friends, whose work I love, have made it into new Norton anthologies—a fact both exhilarating and unsettling. Tradition is already different for the next generation of writers. What will they make of it all?

Middle-age tempers us, no doubt. We grow more respectful of our elders as we endure adult life and know its weight of choices and losses. I am a more patient, attentive reader of the literary past now. But the fact remains that it will never feel like "mine," like something I need to nod toward, compete with, or try to take my place in. In the nuclear age, the very idea of the on-goingness of tradition is, anyway, riddled with painful irony. So I write, largely, out of a sense of displacement, discontinuity, out of my own peculiar mix of experience and preference. I look most often to the women a step before me. But I learn too from the ambivalence and vulnerability of the most seemingly confident poets of the tradition, those terribly perfect ones, like Yeats, who asserted that "works of art are always begotten by previous works of art," but acknowledged in the end that "all the ladders start,/In the foul rag-and-bone shop of the heart." Or George Herbert, addressing and emulating his angry God, close in tone to how I might address the old anthologies:

> I will complain, yet praise;
> I will bewail, approve;
> And all my sour-sweet days
> I will lament, and love.

NOTES

1. James Wright, "To the Muse," *Shall We Gather at the River*, © 1968 by James Wright, Wesleyan U. Press. Quoted with permission of U. Press of New England.

2. C. S. Lewis, *A Preface to Paradise Lost* (London: Oxford U. Press, 1961), p. 3.

3. Deborah Tall, "Q & A with Eavan Boland," *Irish Literary Supplement* (Fall 1988), p. 39.

4. Edith Södergran, "We Women," trans. Stina Katchadourian, *Love & Solitude: Selected Poems 1916-1923* (Seattle: Fjord Press, 1992), p. 51. Quoted with permission of the publisher.

5. Reprinted from Keith Basso, *Western Apache Language and Culture: Essays in Linguistic Anthropology* (Tucson: U. of Arizona Press, © 1990), pp. 153-54. Quoted with permission of the publisher.

6. Eavan Boland, "The Woman Poet: Her Dilemma," *American Poetry Review*, Vol. 16, No. 1 (Jan./Feb. 1987), p. 20.

7. Liz Rosenberg, in *Taking Note: From Poets' Notebooks*, ed. S. Kuusisto, D. Tall, and D. Weiss (Geneva, N. Y.: Hobart and William Smith Colleges Press, 1991), p. 196.

WENDY BATTIN is the author of *In the Solar Wind*, a National Poetry Series selection. Her poems have appeared in *Yale Review, Gettysburg Review, The Nation, Massachusetts Review*, and many other magazines and anthologies. She has received fellowships from the National Endowment for the Arts, the Ingram Merrill Foundation, and the Fine Arts Work Center in Provincetown, and has been a winner of the Discovery/*The Nation* Award and of *River City*'s Hohenberg Award. She teaches at Smith College.

EAVAN BOLAND is the author of five volumes of poetry. *Outside History: Selected Poems 1980-1990* was published by Norton in 1990. Her poems have appeared in *The Atlantic Monthly, The New Yorker, Partisan Review, American Poetry Review*, and numerous other publications. Her awards include grants from the Irish Arts Council and the Ingram Merrill Foundation. She lives in Ireland.

SHARON BRYAN is the author of three collections of poetry: *Salt Air, Objects of Affection*, and *Belongings*. Her awards include a Discovery/*The Nation* Award and a National Endowment for the Arts fellowship. She will serve as Poet-in-Residence at The Frost Place in 1993. She teaches at Memphis State University and is the editor of *River City*.

AMY CLAMPITT'S books of poetry include *The Kingfisher, What the Light Was Like, Archaic Figure*, and *Westward*. She has received fellowships from the Guggenheim Foundation and the Academy of American Poets, and is a member of the National Institute of Arts and Letters. She has taught at the College of William and Mary, Amherst, Washington University, and Smith. She lives in New York City.

MARTHA COLLINS is the author of three books of poetry: *The Catastrophe of Rainbows* (Cleveland State, 1985); *The Arrangement of Space* (Gibbs Smith, 1991); and *A History of Small Life on a Windy Planet* (Georgia, 1993), which won the Alice Fay Di Castagnola Award for work-in-progress. Other awards include a Pushcart Prize and fellowships from the National Endowment for the Arts, the Ingram Merrill Foundation, and the Bunting

Institute. She has also edited a collection of essays on Louise Bogan, published 1984. She is co-director of the creative writing program at the University of Massachusetts-Boston.

MADELINE DEFREES'S poems, short stories, and essays have appeared widely during the past fifty years, some of them under the name of Sister Mary Gilbert during the thirty-eight years she spent as a nun. She is the author of six books of poems, most recently *Imaginary Ancestors* (Broken Moon Press, 1990); *The Light Station on Tillamook Rock* (Arrowood Books, 1991); and *Possible Sibyls* (Lynx House Press, 1991). She has received fellowships from the Guggenheim Foundation and the National Endowment for the Arts. She taught for six years at the University of Massachusetts, Amherst, and has since served as Distinguished Poet-in-Residence at Bucknell University, Eastern Washington University, and Wichita State University. She lives and works in Seattle.

KATHLEEN FRASER is a poet, essayist, and founder/editor of the journal *HOW(ever)*. She was Professor of Creative Writing at San Francisco State University (1972-1992), where she directed The Poetry Center from 1973 to 1976 and founded The American Poetry Archive. Her forthcoming collection, *When New Time Folds Up* (CHAX), will be published in Fall 1993 and her *Collected Poems, 1966-1992* will be published by the National Poetry Foundation in 1994. She lives in Rome for five months a year and is currently translating the work of several Italian women poets.

DEBORA GREGER is the author of three collections of poetry, *Movable Islands* (1980), *And* (1986), and *The 1002nd Night* (1990), published by Princeton University Press. She has received the Peter I. B. Lavan Younger Poets Award from the Academy of American Poets, the Award in Literature from the American Academy and Institute of Arts and Letters, and the Brandeis University Award in Poetry. She teaches in the Creative Writing Program at the University of Florida.

JOY HARJO'S books include *What Moon Drove Me to This?*, *She Had Some Horses*, and *In Mad Love and War*. She has received an Academy of American Poets prize, a National Endowment for the Arts fellowship, and an Arizona Commission on the Arts creative writing fellowship. She lives in Tucson.

GWEN HEAD'S new and selected poems, *Frequencies: A Gamut of Poems*, was published by the University of Utah Press in 1992. Her two previous books were *Special Effects* and *The Ten Thousandth Night*. She is publisher and founding editor of Dragon Gate Press, and has taught at the Iowa Writers' Workshop, the University of California at Davis, and Aspen, Park City, and Port Townsend writers' conferences. She lives in Berkeley.

BRENDA HILLMAN is the author of a chapbook, *Coffee 3 A.M.*, published by Penumbra Press, and four full-length collections: *White Dress, Fortress, Death Tractates*, and *Bright Existence*, all from Wesleyan University Press. Her awards include the Delmore Schwartz Memorial Award and the Silver Medal from the Commonwealth Club. She teaches at St. Mary's College in Moraga, California.

JUDITH KITCHEN teaches at SUNY Brockport and is currently the regular poetry reviewer for *The Georgia Review*. Her essays have appeared in such magazines as *The Georgia Review, The Gettysburg Review, Prairie Schooner,* and *River City*. She was awarded a Pushcart Prize in creative nonfiction in 1990 and a fellowship in poetry from the National Endowment for the Arts in 1991. She is the author of *Perennials* (poems, Anhinga Press) and *Understanding William Stafford*. She serves as editor for the State Street Press chapbook series.

MAXINE KUMIN is the author of ten books of poems; her most recent collection, *Looking for Luck* (W. W. Norton & Co.), was a finalist for the National Book Critics Circle Award. She won the Pulitzer Prize in Poetry in 1973 for *Up Country*. She has also written four novels, a collection of short stories, and two essay collections. She lives on a farm in New Hampshire.

CYNTHIA MACDONALD'S latest book, *Living Wills: New and Selected Poems* (Knopf, 1991) was chosen as a recommended book of poetry by *The New York Times* in its year-end round-up. Her grants and awards include three National Endowment for the Arts grants—two for poetry, one for an opera libretto—Guggenheim and Rockefeller fellowships, and an award from the American Academy and Institute of Arts and Letters. In 1992 she received the Folger Shakespeare Library's O. B. Hardison Prize. She lives in Houston, where in 1979 she founded the creative writing program in which she now teaches. She also has a psychoanalytic practice specializing in treating people who suffer from writing blocks.

SUZANNE MATSON's books of poetry include *Sea Level* (1990) and *Durable Goods* (forthcoming in Fall 1993), both from Alice James Press. Her poems have appeared in *American Poetry Review, Boston Review, Indiana Review, Poetry, Poetry Northwest, Shenandoah,* and others. She has essays out or forthcoming in *Mid-American Review, Denver Quarterly, Harvard Review,* and *American Poetry Review.* Her awards include an Academy of American Poets prize and the Young Poet's Prize from *Poetry Northwest.* She teaches in the English department at Boston College.

COLLEEN J. MCELROY is the author of eight books of poems, including *What Madness Brought Me Here: Selected Poems, 1968-89.* She is also the author of two collections of short fiction, the most recent of which is *Driving Under the Cardboard Pine.* She has received an American Book Award, a Fulbright fellowship, a National Endowment for the Arts fellowship, and a grant from the Rockefeller Foundation. She is Professor of English at the University of Washington in Seattle.

LISEL MUELLER's most recent collection of poetry is *Waving from Shore.* She is the author of four other collections, including *The Need to Hold Still,* which won the 1981 National Book Award. She is also a translator from the German, with special emphasis on the prose and poetry of the twentieth-century writer Marie Luise Kaschnitz.

CAROL MUSKE has two new books from Viking/Penguin: *Red Trousseau,* her fifth book of poems, and *Saving St. Germ* (as Carol Muske Dukes), her second novel. She has been the recipient of an Ingram Merrill grant, a National Endowment for the Arts fellowship, and a Guggenheim fellowship. She is a professor of English at the University of Southern California.

ALICIA OSTRIKER is a poet and critic. Her poetry collections include *Lover,* which won the 1986 William Carlos Williams Award from the Poetry Society of America, and *Green Age* (1989). Her critical work includes *Vision and Verse in William Blake* and an annotated edition of Blake's *Complete Poems* (Penguin). She has also published *Writing Like a Woman* (1983) and *Stealing the Language: The Emergence of Women's Poetry in America* (1986). Her most recent book is *Feminist Revision and the Bible* (1993). She lives in Princeton, New Jersey, and teaches English and creative writing at Rutgers University.

PATTIANN ROGERS has published four volumes of poetry, two of which, *The Expectations of Light* and *Splitting and Binding*, won the Texas Institute of Letters Award for poetry. Her fifth book, *Geocentric*, appeared in 1993 from Gibbs Smith, and her *New and Selected Poems* will appear from Milkweed Editions in 1994. She has received two National Endowment for the Arts fellowships, a Guggenheim fellowship, and Lannan fellowship. Her poetry has won four Pushcart Prizes, as well as the Bess Hokin Prize and the Eunice Tietjens Prize from *Poetry*, the Roethke Prize from *Poetry Northwest*, and the Strousse Award from *Prairie Schooner*. She is the mother of two grown sons and presently lives with her husband in Castle Rock, Colorado.

GRACE SCHULMAN'S poetry collections include *Burn Down the Icons* and *Hemispheres*, and she is completing a new manuscript tentatively titled *After the Division*. She is the author of a critical study, *Marianne Moore: The Poetry of Engagement*, and has published several translations of poetry books. Her poems, articles, and translations have appeared in many literary journals and magazines. She is poetry editor of *The Nation*, and a former director of the Poetry Center, 92nd Street Y.

ANNE STEVENSON, born in England of American parents, was educated at the University of Michigan in Ann Arbor, where she won a Hopwood Award for poetry in 1954. A resident of Britain since 1962, she has been a fellow of Lady Margaret Hall, Oxford, and writer-in-residence in Reading, Dundee, Newcastle/ Durham, and the University of Edinburgh. In 1979, with Alan Halsey and Michael Farley, she co-founded The Poetry Bookshop in Hay-on-Wye. Her ten collections of poetry include *Correspondences* (1977), *The Fiction-Makers* (a Poetry Book Society Choice in 1985), *Selected Poems* (1987) and *Four and a Half Dancing Men*, to be published in 1993. A contributor to leading literary journals in Great Britain and America, she has also published a critical study of Elizabeth Bishop and a biography of Sylvia Plath. In 1990 Anne Stevenson received the Athena Award for distinguished women graduates from the University of Michigan.

DEBORAH TALL is the author of three books of poems (most recently *Come Wind, Come Weather* from State Street Press) and two books of nonfiction: *The Island of the White Cow: Memories of an Irish Island* (Atheneum, 1986) and *From Where We Stand: Recovering a Sense of Place* (Knopf, 1993). She edits the poetry journal *Seneca Review* and was co-editor of the collection *Taking Note: From Poets' Notebooks* (1991). She has taught writing and literature at Hobart and William Smith Colleges in Geneva, New York, since 1982, and has won several awards for her work, including a grant from the Ingram Merrill Foundation and a Hopwood Award.